THE KING'S
ENGLISH

The King's English
A Guide to Modern Usage

Kingsley Amis

HarperCollins*Publishers*

HarperCollins*Publishers*
77–85 Fulham Palace Road
Hammersmith, London, W6 8JB

Published by HarperCollins*Publishers* 1997

Copyright © The Estate of Kingsley Amis 1997

1 3 5 7 9 8 6 4 2

A catalogue record for this book is
available from the British Library

ISBN 0 00 255681 2

Set in Postscript Garamond No. 3 by
Rowland Phototypesetting Limited
Bury St Edmunds, Suffolk

Printed and bound in Great Britain by
Caledonian International Book Manufacturing Ltd, Glasgow

Contents

Preface

This book is intended partly as a work of definition and reference, in which some modern linguistic problems are discussed and perhaps settled, and partly as a collection of more or less discursive essays on linguistic problems. In no sense is it complete or exhaustive. Even the great predecessor of the present volume, the *Modern English Usage* of H.W. Fowler, never set out to be that. What Fowler's aim was takes some defining. To settle scores as well as problems, to shake things up, to make people think about what they said and wrote, to be provocative without being unjust, these were certainly among his aims. In my less educated way they are among mine.

Fowler reprinted hundreds of real examples of real misuses. To have done so lends his work an authoritativeness mine does not attempt to match. For all that, 'a feigned example hath as much force to teach as a true example,' and what the editor has fabricated may make up in concentration and aptness for what it fails to include. Chapter and verse is not much of an extra deterrent, and the parable of the Prodigal Son would not have been more effective if it had named names.

All talk of deterrence may be beside the point. Despite his sometimes derisive and even caustic tone, one easily guesses that Fowler had no real hope that his recommendations would be followed by more than a small fraction of his readership. No writer on the subject can nourish such a hope. The most that can be offered is some guidance for those who may want it and the thought that, without Fowler and his heirs and allies, the language might be in an even worse state than it is. A lost cause may still deserve support, and that support is never wasted.

Apologia Pro Vita Sua Academica

My interest in words as parts of language preceded their appeal to me as units of literature of any sort, and I was learning how to spell some individual words before I knew what they meant. Ever since, I have retained what I like to think of as a special feeling for language in spoken as well as written form. This has gone hand in hand with one of the less immediately appealing sides of my character, the didactic or put-'em-right side. I would guess that for every acquaintance of mine who looks on me as some sort of authority on correct usage or pronunciation there is at least one who sees me as an officious neurotic who sets right venial blunderers uninvited. Any vocal stickler for accuracy perpetually runs that sort of risk.

Turning now to more material things, I was educated more formally than has since been common. I was taught to analyse sentences, to identify subject, verb and predicate and to separate subordinate clauses from the main clause. I had studied general English, as it was called at the time, and was thought good at it. From the age of ten or so, along with millions of my school-fellows, I was taught Latin and, less formally, French. From the age of twelve I was educated in these two languages and in classical Greek. Although the writing of Latin and Greek proses and verses was part of every classical scholar's curriculum, the practice of doing so was far less an exercise of any literary imagination than a means of acquiring proficiency in those tongues and their grammars. Nevertheless, for reasons that may emerge in later parts of this book, I regard these exercises as excellent training for composition in one's own language, whether verse or prose, and for any closer investigation of that language. I miss close contact with the literature of a living language other than English and consider myself impoverished by this lack.

At university I studied, lazily I fear, the early history of our language and some of the works written in it before the year 1500. Perhaps misguidedly and, not only in my case, certainly in vain, our teacher encouraged us to find emotion and even merit in the likes of *Beowulf* and 'The Dream of the Rood'. It would have been better all round if this part of the course had been separated off and introduced under another and un-ashamedly philological heading and literary considerations dropped.

Thereafter I took an interest in linguistic matters that was sometimes close, as at the publication of a new volume supplementing the *OED*, but never expert or professional. This interest has continued to the present day, not surprisingly in the case of a living language that, like all such, is continuously changing. Occasionally I think that a kind of training that has not for many years been more than avocational is no real training at all, is one that fits its recipients better for argufying than for argument, and am suitably chastened. Not for long: I spot some fresh linguistic barbarism and am off again. I am sustained by reflecting that the defence of the language is too large a matter to be left to the properly qualified, and if I make mistakes, well, so do they, and we must carry on as best we can pending the advent of a worthy successor to Fowler.

Bibliography

This book should probably be read alongside other books, with those other books physically handy and often open, though I should not want to lose any reader in search of entertainment or simple information. What I give here is less a bibliography in the recommended-reading sense than a talkative list of those other books that I found indispensable or at least useful in writing this one.

1. *Dictionaries. The Oxford English Dictionary (OED).* The beginnings of that enormous work can be traced back to 1857, in which year the Philological Society heard two significant papers delivered by one of its members. The *Dictionary* itself, serially published over the years 1864–1928, contains articles on over 400,000 words and nearly 2 million quotations. It is thus a monument to Victorian scholarship, though unlike many monuments it is still necessary today. Supplements in 1933 and in the 1970s and 1980s have brought the work up to date in so far as this is possible. Any self-respecting writer needs a copy to hand. The miniaturised version, in two volumes with magnifying lens, is tolerable for bare reference only, not for the necessary unmethodical reading.

The *Concise Oxford Dictionary (COD)* was originally published in 1911. The first edition, now hard to come by, was the work of the Fowler brothers (see FOWLER) not only in its words and definitions but also in its innumerable expressions illustrating usage. Many subsequent revised editions and reprints of these have appeared. For this book I have used the fifth edition of 1964 and the seventh of 1982. The 1982 edition is on my desk at all times.

Webster's *International Dictionary* is physically huge but necessary for American usages and spellings and also contains much encyclopedic information of interest to the British reader, who may also find *The American College Dictionary* (orig. 1947) useful.

Other British dictionaries such as those of Chambers, Collins or Longman may be of help and interest, worth keeping on a readily accessible shelf.

2. *Guides to Usage.* This section heading perhaps raises questions of legitimacy, but there can be no doubt about the precedence in the whole field of H.W. Fowler's *Modern English Usage (MEU)*, first published 1926 (see FOWLER). The present book was written with the 1926 work open beside the typewriter and is best read with it similarly accessible. Note now that this adherence to a document compiled so long ago perhaps indicates not just a conservative or even reactionary stance but also a recognition of necessity. In addition it points to the slow rate of linguistic change, whether for good or ill.

The King's English, by H.W. and F.G. Fowler (1906) is mentioned in this position to indicate its lesser usefulness and trenchancy as compared with the later work, but is nevertheless valuable. See FOWLER.

Modern American Usage, by Wilson Follett and others (1966), makes its allegiance clear in its title. In its vigorous fashion it shows, among much else, how little good US linguistic behaviour has come to differ from its British counterpart.

The Complete Plain Words (1954), comprising *Plain Words* and *The ABC of Plain Words*. By Ernest Gowers, revised 1973 by Bruce Fraser, designed to improve official English and published by HM Stationery Office.

Grammar and Style, by Michael Dummett (1993). Written 'for examination candidates and others'.

Daily Mirror Style, by Keith Waterhouse (1980s). Originally a house manual for journalists, this is now available in an expanded version in Penguin under the expanded title *Waterhouse on Newspaper Style* (1993).

3. *Pronunciation.* Most useful: *The BBC Pronouncing Dictionary of British Names* (1983) has unfortunately been out of print since 1990. The paperback is also out of print.

How to Pronounce It, by Alan S.C. Ross (1st edn. 1970). Mainly but not exclusively proper names. To be used with some caution.

For words that are not proper names, *COD*'s pronunciations are reliable.

4. *Linguistics.* As I explain elsewhere, I am not a professional or even a trained linguist or linguistician, but I have found some linguistic terms and procedures useful. For this purpose I have many times consulted a volume inherited from my youth, *Language*, by Leonard Bloomfield (1st edn. 1933), especially in search of facts. Bloomfield was a major influence on the development of structural linguistics, I am told, and is now opposed by Noam Chomsky.

5. *Thesaurus.* I can do little here except reiterate the name of Roget, say that my copy of his work sits on my desk with Fowler and the *COD* and add something I have recently noticed, viz. that the presence in its text and index of fashionable solecistic uses shows some sort of widespread acceptance. So the latest edition includes *restauranteur* (*sic*), for instance. (*Pristine* is not listed at all, however, neither in its correct nor its incorrect sense.)

A

-able and -ible

I once wrote deduceable instead of deducible in a book, though nobody then or since has taken me up on it. A small point as they go, perhaps, but Rule 1 of writing acceptably is to get everything right as far as you can, and in this case I had neglected to.

If I were assembling a complete guide to usage I should feel bound to give here a list of *-able* and *-ible* words, but I am not so I do not. Fowler gives a list of '*-ble words not in -able*' with something like 140 adjectives in it. There follow similarly long lists of 'negatives in *-able* not having *-un*', and others of comparable length and function, five such lists in all containing between them a thousand words ending in *-able* and *-ible*. Lists look impressive but their usefulness is limited. Consult a dictionary.

Accentuation

I use this term to refer to the prominence given a spoken syllable by stressing it. So in *hypnosis*, for example, the middle syllable receives accentuation. My hope is to avoid the ambiguity that use of the sometime synonymous *accent* might bring.

There is a tendency with English words to put the accentuation as near the front of a word as possible. This tendency was once strong enough to make a schoolmaster some years ago do his best to pronounce *anticipatory* accentuating its first syllable, a difficult task even with the number of syllables halved, and a noise like *ántsiptry* attempted. More recently the old tendency has been at work on words like *contribute* and *distribute*. Once to all appearance fixed irreversibly as *contríbute* and *distríbute*, these are in unpopular process of becoming *cóntribute* and *dístribute*. Resistance to all linguistic change is obviously a healthy instinct, but perhaps not so much in the present case, and the accentuation *díspute* for the noun, much execrated, seems natural enough, in line with the general tendency of the language to stress noun on first syllable as against verb on second, as in *présent* and *presént*. I predict that all three changes will shortly be established.

American practice in this matter seems, to a British ear, whimsical if not perverse. Sometimes Americans will throw accentuation further forward than we do, on to the first syllable of foreign words like *consommé* and *Dubonnet*, though they might argue that their practice sounds at any rate less defiantly non-French than ours. In the case of the noun *research*, their practice of stressing the first syllable is spreading over here, much to the resentment of conservative or older speakers. This feeling is perhaps misplaced, since the Americans are only following a traditional rule of the language; see remark on *dispute* above.

I am less wonderfully tolerant over the other and opposite American habit of shifting accentuation the opposite way, especially in personal names. This has been going on over here too for a long time: my father had a friend called Mr Barrel or Barrell who understandably stressed his surname on its second syllable. *Bernard*, forename and surname, is perhaps a more typical case: *Bernárd* in USA, *Bérnard* in UK, though the surname is tending to follow US convention over here and the BBC lays it down. But then the BBC also lays down that the surname *Bottome* — a pseudonym, strange to relate — should be stressed on the second syllable. In fact, both *Bottome* and *Botham* are cosmeticised forms of the old English word *bottom*, for centuries nothing to do with anyone's posterior, signifying a valley or its floor, found in surnames and meaning 'dweller in the valley' (cf. *Wood*, *Hill*, *Holt*, etc.) and in place-names like *Six Mile Bottom*.

To resume briefly: my tolerance wears thin when I hear an accentuation that seems to me wilfully or absurdly eccentric, as when an American in the flesh, no broadcaster he but a decent young fellow, came up with the surname *Fussell*, an English name, stressed in the American way, which I happen to know is not the stress given it by the American writer of that name. (Does the young fellow talk about *Bertránd Russéll?*) And it – my tolerance – snapped altogether the other day when I heard an English broadcaster refer to Shakespeare's *Romeo and Juliet* with *Juliet* given last-syllable-stress treatment. What next? *Antony and Cleop'trah?* See also AMERICANISMS.

Adaptation, adaption

The term *adaption*, presumably made in the first place on strong analogy with *adoption*, is driving out the older and perhaps more correct *adaptation*, especially on literary fringes. Publishers and suchlike will talk to authors about possible *adaptions* of their novels, etc., for the screen or stage. If only to reduce imputations of illiteracy, I mean to continue with *adaptation* for the moment, but the time will probably come when it will seem first quaint and then unintelligible. Sensible people will have switched to *adaption* before then, as they are already switching to *retraction* (rather than *retractation*).

I ask for Glenmorangie malt whisky stressing the third syllable of the name, even though I happen to know the head man there stresses the second, because a rational being

prefers being understood, and served, to being right. No
contest if the place serves The Macallan.

Address

Near the end of his enjoyable piece, 'Politics and the English
Language' (1946), George Orwell gives six rules for decent
writing 'that one can rely on when instinct fails'. They are
not infallible, these rules, as he would have agreed, but
no. 1 has a great deal to be said for it:

> Never use a metaphor, simile or other figure of speech
> which you are used to seeing in print.

Adherence to this prohibition would certainly cut down the
tedious incidence of *addressing* this, that and the other, of
addressing a question, a problem, a situation, a difficulty
that requires to be faced in defiance of the many attempts
to sweep it under the carpet, confronting most newspaper
readers most mornings. As so often, both reader and writer
are helped to feel that some progress is made towards handling, even solving, a question or problem merely by mentioning it. A really fresh approach calls for fresh words, and
without them silence is at least fairer.

Aggro

This colloquialism, already showing signs of age, can be
taken as descending partly from *aggression* and partly from
aggravation in the colloquial, improper sense of *annoyance*,
exasperation. It is often decried, but in its striking of the
balance between the two in expressions like *I kept away
because I couldn't stand the thought of all the aggro* it has or had
its niche in the informal vocabulary. Plenty of disreputably

descended words and persons have found a tolerated if not a welcome place in this country, to risk sounding pompous.

Albeit

This word is perhaps not felt by its occasional users to be an archaism and probably not felt either to be just a fancy variant of *though* or *although*. It can carry a sense of special understanding and indulgence missing from the more ordinary conjunctions, as in, it might be, 'He was not seriously annoyed, albeit a trifle irritated, that she left without saying good night' – not annoyed, just, well, it might have been silly of him but he couldn't help feeling a little put out that she left, etc. Not the sort of thing we hope to find in our sort of book, maybe, but surely innocuous enough. And it is right, or at any rate understandable, to be impatient with *anent* and *aught* and *perchance*, but to write an occasional *albeit* never did anyone much harm if an eye was kept on the tendency.

Ale

Fowler is right so much of the time that it is a guilty pleasure to correct him on those rare occasions when insufficient knowledge on his part or a change in circumstances has shown him to be wrong. So in writing of *ale* and *beer* he asserts that 'in ordinary use, as at table, both denote the same thing, including the pale and excluding the dark varieties of malt liquor; the difference is that *beer* is the natural current word, and *ale* is' a horrible thing called a Genteelism, like *stomach* for *belly*. (See BELLY and GENTEELISM.) No longer true, if ever. It remains the case that only a fearful fellow would ask, say, if you would care for a glass of *ale* with your ham sandwich, but the two drinks

5

are distinct, *ale* being the result of a fermentation of malt, and *beer* being the same thing flavoured with hops (or ginger, etc.). *Malt liquor*, especially in the USA, became the name for an extra strong ale.

Allergic

Allergy is an unusual sensitivity to the action of particular substances or foods, such as gluten or shellfish, that are harmless to normal people. The reaction can be serious as well as distressing. It is perhaps yobbish to say one is *allergic* to certain people when all that is meant is that they get on one's nerves.

All right

I hope I need not say that this is the correct form, making two separate words of it. The one-word travesty, *alright*, was said in the A–G volume of the Supplement to *OED* in 1972 to be 'a frequent spelling of *all right*'. Yet the citation there of most recent date is taken from *MEU* of 1926, where Fowler says, in part, that *alright*, 'if seldom allowed by the compositors to appear in print, is often seen . . . in MS'.

Fowler never said anything without good reason, and I can testify personally that in my schooldays before the Second War *alright* was indeed often seen – and nearly as often derided. I remember part of a solemn condemnation that ran, '*Alright* is always and altogether all wrong,' and the incorrect form became nearly as much a favourite target of popular scorn as *get* in the sense of 'obtain' or 'become'. Perhaps this did the trick; something did, anyway, for *alright* is very seldom seen nowadays. Its appearance in the title of an amusing television show of the 1990s, *It'll be*

Alright on the Night, a succession of embarrassingly spoilt takes, may seem a conscious barbarism. Even so there will perhaps be many whom it offends.

I am one of them. No doubt as fully aware as most people that language is nothing but a series of signs to convey meaning, and that in this sense no damage seems to be threatening any part of our existing arrangements, I still feel that to inscribe *alright* is gross, crass, coarse and to be avoided, and I now say so. Its interdiction is as pure an example as possible of a rule without a reason, and in my case may well show nothing but how tenacious a hold early training can take.

Also

This word, as Fowler properly reminds us, is indeed an adverb and not a conjunction, but it would be dull to forbid its conjunctional use altogether. Grammatical rules do not apply so strictly to comic writing and dialogue. A vernacular style can very readily produce boring or offensive results, but no amount of grammar would alleviate that.

Alternate(ly) and alternative(ly)

There is no excuse but the grossest similarity in appearance to confuse these two, but people muddle them up all the time. *Alternately* means 'first one, then the other, then the one, then the other, and so on'; *alternatively* means 'another possibility is that . . .' Similarly with the adjectives *alternate* and *alternative*.

Since *alternative* already contains the sense of 'another possibility', it is saying things twice over to speak of 'another alternative'. Remember that Mrs Thatcher said, 'There is no alternative,' not 'There is no *other* alternative.'

7

Exception: An Americanism that sounds anomalous to British ears, as Americanisms will, is contained in the phrase 'alternate world' and its derivatives. This refers to a kind of science-fiction story or idea whereby some great crisis of the past went the other way and correspondingly changed history since that point. Thus a favourite speculation involves a world in which the South won the American Civil War. British readers are advised to follow this trend in the science-fiction context and nowhere else.

Americanisms

I open this large subject by declaring that in almost all political and social matters I am strongly pro-American. So I should be, considering how much I owe America and Americans. Thanks to them I enjoyed one of the best years of my life in 1958–9, mainly at Princeton University; everybody who served alongside US forces in the Second World War has reason to respect them; I thank country and people for many hundreds of hours of pleasurable entertainment; two of the art-forms that have meant most to me, jazz and science fiction, have a strong claim to be American creations. And every British person, along with other millions, has America and Americans to thank for life and liberty.

Any American who might happen to be reading this could be forgiven for mentally preparing to receive an emphatic 'but' followed by an uproar of objurgation. Here I hope to disappoint such anxiety a little. Let me at once affirm something that takes us a little closer to matters of language and is the best test of the sincerity of what I have been saying. As I wrote in 1985, apart from being a politidate, the year 1776 is

a good marker for the point or stage at which English ceased to be solely the language of the inhabitants of the

United Kingdom [and their progeny] and became also that of autonomous speech-communities round the world.

The vital, all-conceding word here is 'autonomous'. In his heart, and however he may vote, no Englishman readily allows linguistic equality to an American or anyone else born outside these shores. Not even this Englishman allows it readily, and I take that as evidence of a sound conservative instinct. Nevertheless it must bow to history and reality.

As a matter of fact, many Americanisms, that is terms or usages originating in America, are embedded so deeply in British speech and writing that they are no longer thought of as such. This tendency goes back a long way. In 1789, Benjamin Franklin sent Noah Webster a list of unauthorised words that should carry 'a discountenancing mark' in his eventual *American Dictionary of the English Language* (1828). These included such barbarous coinages as *noticed* as a verb and *advocate* and *progress* also as verbs, also *opposed* ('tho' not a new word'). Rather later, Edgar Allan Poe apologised for using the word *richness*, a forcible term he says, borrowed from 'colloquy', i.e., one supposes, American conversation.

This catalogue could be much extended. A list of fully assimilated English words and expressions that started life as American coinages or revivals would include *antagonise*, *anyway*, *back-number* (adjectival phrase), *back yard* (as in nimby), *bath-robe*, *bumper* (car), *editorial* (noun), *fix up*, *just* (=quite, very, exactly), *nervous* (=timid), *peanut*, *placate*, *realise* (=see, understand), *reckon*, *soft drink*, *transpire*, *wash-stand*.

In some cases, Americanisms have driven out a native equivalent or are in process of doing so. For instance, in no particular order, *ad* has pretty well replaced *advert* as an abbreviation for *advertisement*, a Press *clipping* is driving out *cutting* as a piece taken from a newspaper, *a whole new ball-game*, that is a metaphorical game of baseball, is what meets

9

the harried circumspect eye where once *a different kettle of fish* or *a horse of another colour* furnished the challenge, and someone *quit* his job where not so long ago he *quitted* it.

Such matters probably indicate nothing more than minor, harmless linguistic interchange, with a bias towards American modes of expression as likely to seem the livelier and (to adopt an Americanism) smarter alternative. I feel less sanguine about the loss of *fortnight* to the American *two weeks* (as soon say *sennight* and expect to be understood), the new voicing of the second syllable in words like *version* (heard now as *verzh'n*) and the adoption of American stress in *research* (noun) and *harass* and *harassment*. American influence is busily eroding a valuable and once firm distinction in British speech and writing between, e.g., *I do not have* and *I have not got*, which described different sets of circumstances. For some discussion of this point, see GET, GOT.

The Fowler brothers, H.W. and F.G., in their magisterial work *The King's English* (1906), wrote: 'The English and the American language and literature are both good things; but they are better apart than mixed.' I find it hard to disagree with that, even though it comes at the end of a paragraph mildly denouncing Kipling's vocabulary as Americanised, an objection few would even understand today. I also find it hard to say why I broadly agree with the Fowlers' recommendation, at least as far as 'the American language' is concerned; with some exceptions in science fiction and other genres I have small difficulty in avoiding anything that could be called American literature. I feel it is unnatural, not I think entirely because it uses a language that is not mine, however closely akin to my own. If I say the result seems to me affected, I mean not that American writers are somehow not fully in earnest, and certainly not that they are any more or less affected than the ones over here. To get at what I do mean I need an Anglicism (not, be it noted, a Briticism, which word is an Americanism and a *vox barbara* to boot).

What I and other non-Americans want to say to American novelists and poets is *Come off it*, off your stilts, off your high horse. Be natural for a change, which is not the same thing as being colloquial or writing in a 'pure' style, but beware of writing in any special writing way, a way that you would never speak. Writers seldom write just as they speak, but they move away from their speaking voice at their peril.

There are of course plenty of British writers who write in affected or unnatural modes and styles: Graham Greene and Anthony Burgess are two leading twentieth-century ones at whom one longs to bawl instructions to come off it. Both seem to me to write in non-English ways, though not in American ways; both are mannerists. In P.G. Wodehouse's best vein, that of the Wooster—Jeeves stories, the come-off-it reaction is an indispensable part of the fun. Such a thing could never happen with an American writer, except perhaps at the level of Artemus Ward.

As everybody knows, an American style is not one thing or even a dozen but very many more. I will however mention here two of the larger, the highly oral, colloquial manner of some New York novelists and journalists, and the most literary, abstract, formal approach seen in academic and didactic prose. We ought to be selectively hospitable to the first of these, which has already given us handy terms like *baby-sitter*, *blurb* and *commuter* and space-savers like *spin-off* and *one-off*, all of which have ceased to strike us as American at all. If the greater Americanisation of our speech seems undesirable, we can adopt a policy of not using an expression we recognise as an Americanism except for some particular reason. This is not so very different from the first half of Pope's piece of advice to those considering their choice of words and expressions:

> Be not the first by whom the new are tried,
> Nor yet the last to lay the old aside,

and he could have added, 'if you want to be understood as clearly and universally as possible.'

The other American style I have singled out, the discursive, is not far off being the opposite of the first. Certainly I think I detect a firm preference for the abstract word over the concrete. Here, at any rate, 'American influence is not only pernicious but pervasive,' to quote one commentator, and the following is a typical sample:

> The establishment of minimum constraints for an optimisation of free growth combining elements of user-design for both the individual and the community, forms the basis of this project. The basic order devised is intended to establish a democratic interchange between human and technological factors. The order devised will stimulate multiplicity, multiformity, micro and macro relations: all expressed through logically derived dimensional and functional modules themselves articulated by a system of guiding lines.

Come off it, indeed, but off what exactly? That paragraph means nothing much at all – I should have said there is in it a minimalisation of semantic and referential content-material. But after some thought it seems hard to blame this kind of thing exclusively or even chiefly on American example and influence. At least as much love of long words and sheer windy pomposity is to be found over here. Nevertheless American and not British English has become the international language, and it has specifically become the language of the United Nations and its agencies and their published literature. What one is objecting to is really committee English, and there is not a lot to be done about that, as about many other unpleasant things, bar making and keeping an individual vow not to add to it oneself.

Amongst

Formerly a variant of *among* permitted and even encouraged in certain contexts – cf. *while* and *whilst*. Both longer forms are still recognisable, but not to be used unless a fussy, old-fashioned air should for some reason be aimed at. *Although* is less handy and versatile than *though*, but may still be preferred in rather more formal situations, especially at the beginning of a sentence of some length.

And

This little word is one of the most troublesome in the language and one of the most often misused. Its proper use is not taught at any school I have ever heard of and most people go into the great world with no more than a vague impression that *and* is used in sentences to link together many things, especially perhaps the last two words in a list, as in *They serve peas, beans and carrots*. It is not now usual to put a comma after *beans* as well as one after *peas* in such sentences. If the list has only two items, *and* of course links them, as in *They serve peas and carrots*.

This is all very well as far as it goes, but many people seem to draw a false deduction from it, namely that *and* must only be used once in a sentence and pretty near its end for preference. However it comes about, this untruth produces what is very likely the commonest mistake in written English, exemplified in the following sentence:

Samantha is twenty years old, blue-eyed and has a large bust.

The nearest correct version is:

Samantha is twenty years old and blue-eyed and has a large bust.

If we peer closely we see that the writer of the incorrect version thought he was reciting one list of three items, but the correct version shows he was in fact reciting two lists. The first of them consisted of Samantha's age and eye-colour, the second of them of three facts about her, the two already referred to and information about her bust. And the first list no less than the second calls for an *and* to link its parts. If the first list were to be offered on its own, nobody who knew any English and was not trying to be funny would write:

> *Samantha is twenty years old, blue-eyed.*

So it is true that *and* normally appears on a list only once, but to be sure of not going astray the writer needs to be sure how many lists are involved.

I said above that it was 'not now usual' to put a comma before *and* in lists, and this is true enough but calls for a little more to be said. For special emphasis of one sort or another, such a comma can contribute valuably, as in:

> *The guerrillas killed every man, woman, and child in the village.*

And the idea that *and* must not begin a sentence, or even a paragraph, is an empty superstition. The same goes for *but*. Indeed either word can give unimprovably early warning of the sort of thing that is to follow.

Apostrophe

The rules governing the use of this vexing little mark are evidently hard to master, and if you have any trouble with them or it after the age of fourteen or so, the chances are that you will always be liable to error in the matter. Still, the rules are:

1. To mark ordinary plurals (*carrot's, pickle's*), the so-called greengrocer's apostrophe, its use is illiterate. Some people write about *the 1990's*, but I prefer *the 1990s*. Those who mind their *p's and q's* must be tolerated. I have seen an illiterate apostrophe even in the impeccably middle-class setting of a dentist's waiting-room, or rather I have seen its ghost at my own dentist's. A notice on the wall is headed 'Cancellations' in faultless style, and the text begins just as properly, 'Must be made at least twenty-four hours ahead'. But, alas, there is a small smudge before the S of *cancellations* and also that of *hours*, showing where the hand of a literate person has excised an errant apostrophe put there by whoever produced the notice. At the end, it says humbly, 'All we ask is a little thought.'
2. With singular words in the possessive case add *'s* even when the word itself ends in S, as *Jack's bike, the water's edge, Gus's buttonhole.* (A plain apostrophe is added to some words, as in *for Jesus' sake, Keats' poems*, but when in doubt always write the fuller version.)
3. With plural words that end in S just add an apostrophe, as *ladies' room, the Smiths' car.*
4. With plural words that do not end in S, add *'s*, as the *men's room*, the *people's candidate.*

Common errors are:

(a) Putting in an apostrophe where none is needed, as with possessive pronouns such as *its, hers, ours, yours, theirs*; though an apostrophe is required in *one's*.
(b) Putting one in where *e* is needed, as in *the Wales's are estranged* instead of *the Waleses are estranged*.

An accomplished apostrophe-wielder must be able to distinguish instantly between the following:

He is staying with Jones.
He is staying at Jones's.
He is staying with the Joneses.
He is staying at the Joneses'.

Note: Foreign words ending in silent *s* take an extra *'s* in the possessive case, so we get *Legouis's grammar*, *Louis's solo*.

Aren't I?

This is often said but better not written except in fictional dialogue, where it usually helps to characterise some semi-literate or otherwise low person. If it should be written in ordinary prose, *aren't I?* is likely to be categorised as vulgar, or even as not English. It is of course perfectly good English, and in its earlier forms was certainly not vulgar. What follows is of my own devising, but I am aware of no other coherent account of the genesis of *aren't I?*

At some earlier stage in the evolution of our language, certainly before the arrival of mass literacy, speakers of English collectively become aware of a need of some nega-tive-interrogative form for the first person singular present indicative to parallel the handy and easy forms *aren't you*, *isn't he, she, it, aren't we, aren't they*.

The obvious parallel choice was *am not I* or *amn't I*, but nobody could say either easily and the conditions of conversation made them doubly unwieldy. What actually got said was *an't I* or *ain't I*, the latter form certainly recorded.

An't I, its first element originally pronounced to rhyme with modern *pant*, persisted down to the time when the pronunciations of south-eastern England became standard for the whole country. In particular, short A in many words was replaced by long A, and *can't* as a northern speaker might say it today became the familiar *cahn't*. The same thing happened to *an't* as in *an't I*, but English orthography had no way of indicating this except by changing the spelling to *aren't*, with silent R as always in this position in the south-east, and correspondingly *aren't I* started to be written.

That this lineage is at least possible I infer from the now universal form *I won't*, giving *won't I*. Clearly, *I won't* began to establish itself as a colloquial contraction of the first person indicative of the future tense of *I will not* at a time when a lot of people were still saying *I wol not*, last recorded in the sixteenth century; *won't* occurs in the seventeenth (Pepys in 1667), pressure from *wont* (=accustomed) soon lengthening the vowel.

One attraction of my theory is the ill-natured glee it brings to believers in it when they hear some unreconstructed pedant struggling to say *amn't I*. I remember that the late A.J. Ayer was one of these.

Around

I confine myself to British uses, though nowadays these must often be the result of general or particular American example. The *OED*'s first citation is dated '*c* 1300', but goes on to note that it is rare before 1600 and not to be found in Shakespeare or the Authorised Version of 1611. Nevertheless that word continued to be used here as a variant of the more usual *about*, and when H.F. Lyte (1793–1847) wrote in 'Abide with Me' the deservedly famous line:

> Change and decay in all around I see,

nobody would have taken its sixth word for an Americanism. Often, though not in the line quoted, *round* seems to come more naturally to a British speaker, and my rule for the use of *around* would be, stick to *round* and *about* unless *around* strikes you as preferable, and I mean really preferable, not just smarter or trendier or more modern. If you observe that rule you may find yourself using the word less.

As to

This pair of nasty little words has quite lately taken to inserting itself in the phrase 'the question whether' and producing the needless and distasteful variant 'the question as to whether'. The infection has spread to contexts where any indirect question appears, and any moment I expect to read that 'I asked him as to who he was.' So remember, or learn, that twenty thousand Cornish men would know the reason why if Trelawny died, not the reason as to why, and Tennyson said of the Light Brigade troopers that it was theirs not to reason why, not theirs not to reason as to why. Perhaps finally, Cecil Woodham-Smith's great book on the Charge is entitled *The Reason Why* and nothing else.

Aspect

This is the grammatical name given to some categories of verbal form that concern other features of an action than when it is said to take place. This attention to aspect is to be seen in many languages that boast a flourishing tense-system, such as Latin and English. It has often been observed that *amo*, say, means not only *I love* but also *I am loving* and *I do love*, less often perhaps that the first-person present-indicative familiar *amo* can be used to mean anything from still loving away after fifty years to having begun to love that very minute. The durative, the inceptive, the frequentative and all other aspects of an action can be covered in English by means of auxiliary verbs and other periphrases.

This hospitality to aspect as well as tense is one of the things that people mean when they call English a rich language. Latin is more concise and perhaps neater and more accurate, but its structure makes it less finely tuneable in comparison.

Ate

I mean of course the monosyllabic preterite of the English verb *eat*, not the dissyllabic name of the Greek goddess of criminal folly and (later) avenger of sin. Pronounce et, with a short vowel. To pronounce the word as it is spelt is nothing less than a spelling-pronunciation and therefore an example of pedantry, conscious or unconscious, though in neither case a very evil one.

The recommended pronunciation is the choice of *MEU*, *COD* and Professor A.S.C. Ross, expert on U and non-U among other things.

-athon, -thon

Marathon is the name of the place in Greece where in 490 BC the Greeks beat the invading Persians in a decisive battle. A messenger is supposed to have run all the way to Athens with the news, falling down dead on delivering it, as well he might have done after running nonstop what I had better describe as 42.195 km. That at any rate is the length of the marathon race at the modern Olympic Games. Competitive events demanding comparable endurance were quickly set up, like the so-called *dance marathon* in the USA. This institution may have been in doubtful taste but at least its name and nature were clear enough.

Not as much could be said for what followed, when the second half of the word *marathon* was taken as a sort of verbal building-block when devising names for less edifying activities. A *telethon*, for instance, was a series of telephone calls intended to bully the sufferer into buying goods or contributing to a particular charity. There were things called *sale-a-thons* and even *walkathon-talkathons*.

Not every Americanism deserves to have its credentials carefully examined. Some ought to be shot on sight.

Avid

This over-used word is taken in the 1990s as an up-to-date synonym of 'keen, eager'. So it is among other things, and when somebody writes of somebody being an avid collector of ashtrays or an avid reader of modern poetry, no great harm is done, although the reader may groan a little at the sight of yet another capitulation to herd-instinct. But when somebody writes of an avid golfer or an avid motorist, the reader may remember that *avid* is connected with the noun *avidity* and itself still sometimes denotes physical greed for food or drink, and you can tolerably be described as a greedy collector or reader, though surely not as a greedy golfer or motorist. But this may be pedantry on my part. Still, *avid* has become quite sufficiently one of what Fowler called vogue-words to be unemployable without special care.

B

Ballock

The early uses of this word and its by-form *bollock* go back centuries and are wrapped in discretion. I mention them here only to declare my preference for the more correct-looking *ballock*, and perhaps should not have done so at all, any learned debate on obscenities being unattractive and of doubtful value.

Bath and bathe

There is a potential confusion here which used to be veiled by a sort of vestigial puritanism. In the UK, at least, I bath, I bath myself, I have a bath, making the word rhyme each time with *path*. When I bathe in the sea or bathe my sore foot in a basin, I spell the word differently and pronounce it to rhyme with – what? *Scathe*, perhaps, or *lathe* in the sense of a rotary machine. But what exactly do I do in the USA these days? I *take* rather than *have* a bath, of course, just as I *take* rather than *have* a look at something. But what do I do in the sea or pool? Oh, of course I *swim*, I go for a *swim* even when I cannot progress an inch through the water whatever I do. And I suppose I *bathe* my foot like any Englishman.

Americans solve all problems in their way, even minor linguistic ones.

Because

There are two popular, in the sense of common, mistakes made in speech and in informal prose. Both feature that innocent-looking word *because*, and one type of well-intentioned illiterate says or writes *The reason he smashed the car is because he was drunk*, and the other type, who is not so very different from the first type, says or writes *Just because he was drunk doesn't mean it was all right for him to have smashed the car*. Perhaps it was a vague sense of these dangers that, many years ago now, persuaded a committee chairman of my acquaintance to begin a piece of self-explanation by saying, *The reason being is this*. (General horror ensued.)

These are venial errors, but still errors. Practise saying *He smashed the car because he was drunk* and *The fact that he was drunk doesn't mean it was all right*, etc., and take some care over colloquial sentences with *because* in them. Refrain from starting them till you can see through to the end.

Belly

This word had an impeccable Old English and Middle English pedigree and Old Norse and Old High German cognates, whereas *stomach*, an obvious competitor, comes to us via Old French from Latin and ultimately Greek. Of the two, *belly* is the more natural and obvious, *stomach* the more rarefied and scientific or even pseudo-scientific. Unfortunately *belly* today carries an unmistakable whiff of the ruthlessly hairy-chested, down-to-earth, call-a-spade-a-spade 'frankness' that I for one find more embarrassing. To say 'she burnt her *stomach* sunbathing' may well seem over-delicate; to declare roundly 'I never drink on an empty *belly*' sounds to me like going too far in the opposite direction.

Tastes differ; perhaps I can say without much fear of contra-
diction that both words need handling with care.

Tummy, though dating back to 1868, is of course insuf-
ferably arch when not used as a childish term.

Berks and wankers

Not every reader will immediately understand these two
terms as I use them, but most people, most users of English,
habitually distinguish between two types of person whose
linguistic habits they deplore if not abhor. For my present
purpose these habits exclude the way people say their vowel
sounds, not because these are unimportant but because they
are hard to notate and at least as hard to write about.

Berks are careless, coarse, crass, gross and of what anybody
would agree is a lower social class than one's own. They
speak in a slipshod way with dropped Hs, intruded glottal
stops and many mistakes in grammar. Left to them the
English language would die of impurity, like late Latin.

Wankers are prissy, fussy, priggish, prim and of what
they would probably misrepresent as a higher social class
than one's own. They speak in an over-precise way with
much pedantic insistence on letters not generally sounded,
especially Hs. Left to them the language would die of purity,
like medieval Latin.

In cold fact, most speakers, like most writers left to
themselves, try to pursue a course between the slipshod
and the punctilious, however they might describe the
extremes they try to avoid, and this is healthy for them and
the language.

Billion

Until about twenty years ago, the word *billion* meant, in the United Kingdom, one million million or 1,000,000,000,000 or 10^{12}, and in the United States and elsewhere one thousand million or 1,000,000,000 or 10^9. I am not saying which I think is the better system, merely that there were two distinct systems as stated. Then some time in the 1970s the United Kingdom system was changed to bring it into conformity with the US system. I think this change has bewildered many people here, has not been properly taken in by them. Very large numbers with a lot of noughts at the end are always hard to appreciate, and British newspaper readers have not been helped by the practice of printing such unpronounceables as *£816m* and *£.816bn*. No doubt it is too late for us to try to insist on £816,000,000, but surely not to try to insist on printing *£1,000 million*. Otherwise we are in effect conniving at a conspiracy to keep voters in the dark about just what enormous sums are being spent or discussed in their name. And their name includes our name.

Bonus

Used to mean *additional benefit*. Then quite recently lazy and ignorant writers, perhaps foggily remembering or hearing that *bonus* was a Latin word meaning *good* (adjective: a *good thing* would have to be *bonum*), started to write about *an added bonus*, thus with unconscious ineptitude saying *additional* twice over. Who cares? Only you and me and the occasional reader.

Brave

When a child is described in the popular Press as *brave*, we know at once that he or she is near death's door. There may be several reasons for bestowing this invariable description, of which perhaps the worthiest can be traced to a desire to hearten child, family and friends without extreme concern for the facts, should any be discernible in such a case. To carp may seem churlish or worse, but I wonder whether it might not be found acceptable to point out that there are such things as degrees of courage, and that to commend somebody automatically and indiscriminately reduces the value of the commendation. I think I see how difficult it would be to alter what has become a tradition. At the same time I hope no one concerned will notice the merely comforting aspect of it.

Breathalyse(r)

This is just the sort of word that turns an old-fashioned grammarian scarlet with rage. Nevertheless everyone uses it and understands it immediately.

Many years ago, old A.P. Herbert devised a little four-part test for 'new' words, those fancied to be presenting themselves for admission to the language. This entrance exam comprised four questions: Understood? – Can we admire you? – Are you good? (i.e. are your etymological credentials in order?) – Do we require you? A word had to score a minimum of twenty out of a possible forty to get in. *Television*, I remember, scraped by with just twenty, its answers scoring 10—0—0—10. So it has been with *breathalyse* and *breathalyser*. But of course, like *television*, they had already got in by passing the one test that counts, general acceptance; a crude test, no doubt, and yet imposs-ible to fudge or cancel.

Briton

This unsatisfactory* word has come to be used, chiefly in newspapers, to mean 'person of either sex either originating in Great Britain or having acquired British nationality', which is admittedly quite a lot for one short dissyllable. Among its troubles is that, in the sense just given, it is artificial, not natural, a fact reflected in its never appearing in ordinary conversation. Another trouble is that the word refers not to a country or nation but to a geographical feature, the island of Great Britain. (Note for huffy Americans and others: the 'Great' is not a claim to grandeur or importance but to mark the difference between *Grande Bretagne* and *Bretagne*, that is Brittany. Cf. *Great Bear*, etc.) A third such objection says that *Briton* has no resonance or possible appeal to national pride of the sort felt not only by Englishmen but by the inhabitants of Scotland and Wales. Milton did not write that it was the Almighty's practice to reveal Himself 'first to his Britons'. The word *British* is a little more vibrant but, again, Charles Kingsley did not write that 'twas the hard grey weather that bred 'hard British men'.

It might be good if *Briton* could be confined to the popular Press. Where intra-British differences matter, as in sport, no shame or resentment is felt when things are called by their right names. In other conversational circumstances my own solution is to talk about *English* history etc. and Englishmen unless a Scot or a Welshman happens to be in earshot, when I consider switching. But I remember e.g. that the Armada was beaten without Scottish assistance.

Perhaps *Briton* in the modern sense is more deeply entrenched than sometimes appears. The earliest use of it personally known to me comes in 'The Burial of Sir John Moore after Corunna' by Charles Wolfe (1817), where Moore is said to sleep 'in the grave where a Briton has laid him'. This is perhaps a surprising use by a Dublin student in a poem written in Dublin less than twenty years after the Act of Union between Great Britain and Ireland. Wolfe is of course an English surname, like Moore.

Brochure

This is not just a 'needless variant' of *pamphlet*, though no doubt it is sometimes so used and regarded. Whatever its original meaning in French and in English, it has now developed a handy separable sense as the term for a lavish illustrated hand-out issued free by a university, hotel, firm of decorators or similar facility to attract custom, whereas a *pamphlet* is a mere glorified leaflet, priced but usually unbound, on some uncommercial theme. Words like *brochure*, with their commercial taint, are a natural target for purists.

Brutalise

Once happily and usefully settled in the meaning of 'render brutal', as in 'his experiences in Angola and elsewhere seem to have brutalised him', now perverted by Americans and others to mean 'treat brutally', as in 'he was brutalised by the Angolan police', and rendered unusable.

Bureaucrat

Fowler called this a barbarous formation and would have liked us to say burOHcrat and burOHcracy. Recognising that these pronunciations were unlikely to catch on, he settles for a change of spelling to *burocrat* with other forms to match.

For once I think Fowler's hostility was misdirected.

Bureaucrat is a most useful word, and *COD* inaccurately restricts its application to government and governmental officials. It also pertains to what we might now call quangos and their various members, and the power to call somebody a cultural bureaucrat, for instance, is not one to be lightly surrendered.

The word is often misspelt by those who seem to think it derives from French *beau* rather than *bureau*, and *beaurocrats* come popping up all over the place. It is and was and is likely to remain *bureaucrat*, so spelt and pronounced with stress on the first syllable. Anything else is not only a form of showing off, it may also, however briefly, not be understood.

Busing

No, this head-word is not a colloquial form of *abusing* or anything else but the present participle of the verb *to bus*. As such it is necessary for outlining in small compass a whole educational policy, that of conveying, by bus or other means, pupils of a particular race, religion, etc., to a school deemed more suitable for them than one in the neighbourhood in which they live, quite a lot to be saying in one word.

Nevertheless, *busing*, like the preterite *bused*, is not instantly recognisable as what it is. The conjugation of the present indicative starts recognisably enough *I bus*, not *I buss*, which has to do with kissing, but other forms like *busing* and *bused* may cause temporary confusion in a way that *focusing*, *biased*, etc., seldom do. Consistency and logic are to be sought after where no bad things can result, but this may be one of the places where bad things can result, and perhaps it would be better to plunge in and write *bussing* and *bussed*. I think I would if I had to use the term at all often.

C

Capitals and full stops

Once upon a time everything was straightforward and everything was the same, and you wrote of *the R.A.F.* and *the B.B.C.* and *the U.S.A.* under principles that needed no defining, only demonstration. Then bit by bit modernity started arriving and the full stops started disappearing, but at different speeds and with different degrees of completeness. At one stage it looked as if collections of capital initials that could be and often were pronounced as a word, acronyms as they were very often called, consistently lost their full stops, and we wrote *NATO* and *UNO* and *NASA*, and said *Nato* and *Uno* and *Nasa*, and often-used abbreviations lost their stops too and we got *ie* and *eg* and even *rsm* (in *The Times*), and it seemed as if we were within reach of consistency, that grammarian's dream of perfection. But then some of us noticed that to write *RAF* suggested, often wrongly and perhaps annoyingly, that the writer said *Raf*, and that nobody said *Ira*, and that although everybody was writing *USA* nobody ever said *Ooza* or *Yooza* even in fun, and what about people's initials? Consistency, even a rough rule of thumb, seemed and still seems as far off as ever.

There is luckily an easy way out of this not very pressing problem. It consists of heeding the fact that nobody cares much or even observes what you write in your own fist – in a personal letter, say – and more importantly as regards matter to be published no personal system of uniformity has a chance of surviving translation into print. 'House style' will take care of everything. So go ahead and write *U.S.A.* or *USA* or even *usa* and it will come out the way They want it. N.B. (or NB): This is written not after a tough tussle with printers but in a spirit of detachment and resignation.

More generally, use capitals as little as possible. A particular reference (the Government) earns a capital initial where a general one (any British government) does not. The use of small capitals is also to be encouraged, but that too is a province of house style.

Careful writers

This expression grew current in the permissive years when nobody dared say in so many words that such-and-such an expression was illiterate or wrong, but at the same time people went on feeling that some usages were better than others. Rank barbarisms could not, while that fashion lasted, be denounced as such, only mildly tut-tutted over as 'avoided by careful writers'.

That phrase and concept of course carry on into the present age of renascent prescriptivism, when a spade is coming to be called a spade once more if not yet a bloody shovel. But those careful writers continue as before to avoid the illiteracies and circumvent the dodginesses I have described here. If from time to time they seem to strike a sanctimonious note, to be unduly conscious of their singularity and dedication, this seems a payable price for having such people around. They will persist in fighting the good fight whatever anybody says and under any conditions because they have to, or so it seems to them. Cheered when the general outlook seems good, not unduly dismayed at adverse portents, they pursue good style for its own sake. They know that no linguistic change, large or small, comes about as a result of conscious effort. If Fowler could not discourage the improper use of *eke out* or of *like* as a conjunction, who could?

We have never seen a time when it was fashionable to write well and unfashionable not to, nor are we likely to now that most of us can just about read and write. And even if one did arrive, it would fade away sooner or later, as fashions do. All that can be done is to encourage a few individuals to start thinking about how they express their thoughts. And take care oneself, naturally.

Case

(The grammatical sort, not the noun-use sometimes equivalent to *instance*.)

At first sight the English language has no cases, or only a possessive signalled by apostrophe-S and a couple more in personal and relative pronouns. A little investigation shows that by and large the language has no case-endings, no inflections to show what grammatical job a word is doing in a sentence, and that nevertheless plenty of mistakes can be made that are traceable to a faulty sense of case.

The most common kind of mistake is to use the nominative form of a pronoun where common sense as well as grammar demand an oblique form, and write sentences like:

> Everything good and pleasant in our lives we owe to He that loved us and died for us.

Behind this example there may be a feeling that *He* is posher than *Him* (see remarks on *you and I* in HYPER-URBANISMS), especially in such a solemn context. There is a more widespread feeling that *I* (instead of *me*) and especially *he* (instead of *him*) are always right or suitable before a defining relative clause. Reading the sentence aloud slowly would probably have told the writer that *to He* must be wrong, though nobody with a feeling for words would ever have committed to paper the sentence as it stands.

Nominative where accusative/dative is necessary supplies the vast majority of case-errors in English. But now and then a writer tries to make a noun serve two incompatible purposes, as in:

> There are few things such women value more, or can be more easily resold at a fair price, than the traditional diamond necklace.

Quite a few untrained but observant people will feel uneasy about that sort of sentence, far more than will correctly trace the trouble to the way the word *things* is expected to do two jobs at once, namely to serve as object of the verb *value* and as subject of *can be*, or (if you like) to be switched from the accusative case to the nominative in the same sentence. To be sure, all the grammarian will have done is to identify a fault that many who are not grammarians will have become aware of, but a good half of his trade is giving a name to what other speakers of his language only have a feeling about.

As I write this, there comes handily to hand a letter on the correspondence page of *The Times* newspaper over the names of two persons known to me who share membership of a notorious centre of laxity in London's Covent Garden district. The two write about 'the long-running TV series *Worzel Gummidge* . . . which we developed from the original stories . . . and became something of a cult among adult viewers . . .' Oh dear. The insertion in the right place of a single word (*which*) would have rescued that sentence. Would that all our linguistic difficulties were so readily solved.

Chauvin, chauvinism

Nicolas Chauvin was a soldier of the French Republic and Empire who served under Napoleon Bonaparte and was fanatically devoted to him and his cause. Chauvin soon became a byword for bellicose patriotism, and a character bearing his name was introduced into a number of plays and entertainments, not only in France.

For many years Chauvin and chauvinism, the latter now often printed with a lower-case initial, were domesticated in English as virulent types of jingo and jingoism. More recently, about 1970 in fact, the phrase-makers of the women's rights movement may have noticed that their theories were thin in historicity and colour; anyway, the terms *male chauvinist* and *-ism*, designating the enemy and his 'ideology', began to creep into the language. They had hardly had time to turn round there before the *male* component started to creep out again. Even before the Seventies were over one was running into (female) foes of (male) chauvinism who had never so much as heard of Chauvin. If that kind of person had ever wondered about the Frenchified pronunciation of at any rate the first syllable of *chauvinism* ('show' instead of 'tshaw') no sign of such a thing was discernible. Still, we all know that to be ignorant of the provenance of a word is no bar to using it effectively, and life is short.

Lieut.-Col. Jean Martinet (d. 1672), Louis XIV's inspector-general of infantry, rather similarly had his surname applied to any extreme disciplinarian. He would punish delinquent soldiers with a cat-o'-nine-tails later known as a *martinet*. To this day any severe person in authority is liable to be called a martinet, but the man's name has never been applied to any foe of feminism, real or imagined.

Classic and classical

One would have thought these two were settled down, *classic* used as a noun ('a *classic* of our literature') and as an adjective meaning something like 'standard' or 'ideal' ('a *classic* case of arrested development', 'a *classic* captain's innings'), and *classical* an adjective applied in the first place to styles of art ('a *classical* concerto' as opposed to a baroque or a romantic concerto, '*classical* music' as opposed to light music, jazz, rock, etc.) and to be used instead of *classic* when in doubt.

But then a commercial radio station came along playing records of classical music, or shot bits of it between chatter, and calling itself not Classical FM but Classic FM, one more verbal mistake piled on top of the majestic variety it pours out every minute. The people go wrong by constantly stressing the wrong word and pausing in the wrong place, nothing that a little less laziness would not cure. But that is true of many of the world's ills.

Coastal

A word that 'should be abandoned', says Fowler bluntly, pointing out the fact that the spelling shows by its *oa* that the suffix *-al*, which he finds it unnecessary to state is Latin in origin, has been joined to an English root. *Coastal* itself, however barbarous a formation, goes back to the 1880s and, as few could have foreseen, was to be multiplied millions of times in the Coastal Command of wartime years. Mentioned here chiefly to note that here is another natural prey of purists. Like *television*.

Cohort

In the Roman army a cohort was a squad of infantry that, I now find, could include as many as six hundred men, not far off the complement of a modern infantry battalion under the command of a lieutenant-colonel. A *cohort* today, as in the US President's associates or aides or cohorts described in the media, is or can be something far smaller, a matter of three or four persons or even of one: 'the Senator's *cohort* was smoking a cigarette.' What has brought so much obloquy on this particular misuse is not clear, but it may be the error of nomenclature whereby the meaning of the prefix *co-* has been misinterpreted to signify joint action or close association or cohesion. Anyway, *cohort* has rather mysteriously attracted widespread hostility while *legion*, a division of 3000–6000 combatants, has stood for any large or largeish number without objection for many years.

Colloquial rhythms

It is still said by way of compliment that this or that poet, dramatist, prose writer is good at catching colloquial rhythms, be they those of today or yesterday in Mayfair or Essex or upstate New York. We are all grateful for a word kindly meant, but this one perhaps amounts to less than it may seem.

Every spoken utterance has rhythm in the sense that it consists of a series of syllables variously stressed. This is so essential that an utterance without all rhythm could only be made by a machine of some sort. Every human utterance also has a unique rhythm, even if it repeats in every distinguishable detail another by the same speaker.

All I probably intend to convey is that everything we say or represent as said has its own unique rhythm, one inseparable from its meaning. The rhythm of a sentence cannot be determined if its meaning is ignored or not known. So the rhythm of a sentence like 'I could be reasonably sure he had no strong motive for killing himself' would differ according to which of half a dozen words received emphasis.

And to praise some of Eliot's earlier poems for their ability to catch colloquial or conversational rhythms, as has been done at least once, means either very little or some sort of compliment to their power of rendering in verse colloquial etc. phraseology, spoken expressions. This latter compliment does amount to something. Perhaps it remained unvoiced because, for one reason or another, the writer was shy of claiming knowledge of a kind of phraseology actually in use among the uninstructed.

Connection, connexion

There is a feeling here and there that the spelling of such words with an X is somehow classier, richer in history, *better* than the spelling with CT that everybody naturally adopts. Pfui! Everybody is often wrong but not this time. The philological evidence is dubious and no one has yet succeeded in introducing even the ghost of an X into important by-forms like *connecting*, *connective* and indeed *connect*. So go on writing *connection* and the rest and treating *connexion* and the rest with the tolerant indifference they deserve.

Convince

Another Americanism. Nowadays people will become *convinced to* follow some course of action, whereas until recently they would only become convinced *of* some supposed truth or *that* something was true. The expected form of words was that such people were *persuaded* to do something. I think that that is the reason for the new usage: *persuading* somebody too readily suggests inverted commas, the notion of illegitimate pressure, the use of threats or bribery. A similar process of guilt-by-association has tended to drive out *deny* (see POLITICAL WORDS). To be sure, threats, bribery, etc. are perfectly possible in a case of *convincing* somebody to do something, but that will have to wait.

Crescendo

Once a musical term meaning '(passage played) with increasing volume' and a derived figurative term meaning 'progress towards a climax'. For many years now taken to be a fancy synonym for 'climax' as in 'the gunfire reached a crescendo' or 'the chorus of vilification rose to a crescendo' and rendered usable only by the unwary or vulgar. Outside a strictly musical context, that is.

Crossed 7

To cross one's 7s is perhaps defensible on the Continent, where traditionally people handwrote the numeral 1 with a long upstroke before the downstroke, to distinguish it from the capital letter I. A cross-stroke on the numeral 7 thus distinguishes it from the numeral 1. In English-speaking and other countries where no visible distinction is made between numeral 1 and capital letter I, it is unnecessary and distracting and may be confusing to cross a 7. In less polite language, to do so is either gross affectation or, these days, straightforward ignorance. It should not be tolerated in any person over the age of twelve.

D

Danglers, floaters

> Sheridan was once staying at the house of an elderly
> maiden lady who wanted more of his company than he
> was willing to give. Proposing one day to take a stroll
> with him, he excused himself on account of the badness
> of the weather.

This famous quotation from the earlier nineteenth century
shows that it was then considered quite acceptable to attach
a participle to a main sentence so tenuously as to have
horrified later generations. It was clearly the elderly maiden
lady who proposed the stroll but, far from being the subject
of the second sentence, she appears in the preceding one
and there only in a subordinate capacity. Today, and yesterday too, even a not over-careful writer would have felt
constrained to begin the second sentence with a phrase like
'When she proposed' or 'On her proposing'. This kind of
solecism has begun to attract the dreadful fame of the split
infinitive and the ending of a sentence with a preposition.
This time, however, it is what I (from a lofty pinnacle)
would call a real solecism.

   The dangling participle is not only at least as often committed in America as here, but denounced there at least as
regularly and rudely. In fact it took an American grammarian to point out that the term *dangling participle* is itself
suspect, since a body that dangles is fastened to something

39

firm at one point if nowhere else, as a properly conducted participle is fastened to the subject of a main verb. The *dangling participle*, however, or simply the *dangler*, is the usual term for the thing not only in the USA but increasingly in the UK, where it has virtually driven out Fowler's more strictly accurate but less vivid label, *unattached participle*.

The objection to the unattached or wrongly attached participle is firstly, of course, that it is unprofessional, the sign of a casual or careless writer. Secondly, though not often truly ambiguous, it may cause the attentive reader (the only sort really worth having) to pause without profit, to spend some unnecessary time checking that the sentence in question and its constituent parts are as they seemed to be. There are writers – Shakespeare is one – who can make us pause with profit and decide usefully that something other or more is being said than what first appeared, but they are rare.

In the midst of this scene of warning and prohibition there is fortunately an active class of what have been called acceptable danglers, words that end in *-ing* that have in effect ceased to serve as adjectives and become prepositions or adverbs, like *considering*, which is often used to mean nothing much more than *in view of*. The list of these is long and always growing and includes near its alphabetical beginning words like *assuming* ('assuming this was a typical county side, the proportion of keen fieldsmen seemed unduly low') and *barring* ('barring accidents, they should be home well before dark'). As always, it is up to the writer to decide. *Looking inland*, the snow-capped peaks of the cordillera dominate the prospect, all right? I think not. *Generally speaking?* A virtually unconditional yes.

Data

Yes, by origin plural only, by usage irreversibly singular. Those who write *these data* or *this datum* run the strong risk of being not so much misunderstood as thought to be involved in some misprint muddle. The best solution is to avoid using any form of the word while enjoying a comfortable little thrill of superiority whenever a singular use is spotted. The singular use of *media* is less general so far (1995) but looks likely to prevail; a nice posh-looking term meaning Press plus broadcasting, etc., is obviously handier in the singular than in the plural. I wish only that wits would stop being clever about the pronunciation of the word with a J sound in the middle, surely the original and unpedantic way to say *media*. Some of them even spell the word *meeja*, an excess that perhaps points to a hidden guilt at (mis)using the word in the first place. Compare *agenda*.

Decimate

Decimation was a form of collective punishment in the Roman army, whereby every tenth man in a mutinous or demoralised party of soldiers was executed, so to *decimate* in English was used to mean 'destroy a small but noticeable part of'. Most people would say they know some of that, and yet that useful word has been irreversibly corrupted into just one more synonym for 'damage beyond repair, virtually destroy', but with the advantage of looking rather classy and learned. Not to be used even in the original sense on grounds of ambiguity.

Deism, theism

Deism is belief in any sort of world spirit, a non-personal god who or which unlike other gods has never been revealed to mankind. Theism is belief in a personal, revealed god. Thus Wordsworth, in the Immortality Ode at least, was some kind of deist; the Archbishop of Canterbury is presumably a theist, or is paid to be. By a common error, a person may be labelled a deist when a theist seems to be meant. By a different common error, the first syllable of either word is pronounced to rhyme with *pay* when it should be made to rhyme with *pea*.

Déjà vu, an uncanny sense of

This expression has perhaps been done to death by now. I certainly hope so. Its original application was to a transient psychological state, not uncommon among those under about forty, in which the subject feels that he has seen before some place where he has provably never been in this life (thus providing fanciful evidence for reincarnation). The journalistic contribution has been to apply this feeling to some event or situation a person *has* witnessed before, as just another way of saying that, for instance, a governmental apology for one thing is reminiscent of the same government's apology for another. This added to the world's stock of verbal garbage but it also provided the needy with a useful and quite posh-looking alternative to 'this is where I/we came in' and other tattered phrases with that sort of meaning.

Delusion, illusion

Those already aware of the distinction between these two words and the corresponding states of mind are advised to move to another article. Others may read on.

The only possible source of difficulty is the non-existence of a verb *illude* to contrast with *delude*. In all other respects the differences are straightforward, as straightforward as those between sanity and insanity.

An *illusion* about the world or a part of it may be consciously entertained by a sane person who knows the true state of affairs perfectly well. A *delusion* is fully embraced by someone who to that extent is insane, genuinely convinced of what is not the case.

A sentimental dreamer may enjoy the *illusion* that childhood is a time of beatific happiness; a lunatic may have the *delusion* (however plausible it can seem at times) that children are agents of Satan.

A successful dramatic performance perhaps brings about, via a willing suspension of disbelief, the *illusion* that Hamlet is a real prince of Denmark; another member of the same audience perhaps falls victim to the *delusion* that Claudius is a real villain.

Finally, I cannot improve on Fowler's contradistinction:

That the sun moves round the earth was once a delusion, and is still an illusion.

Destination

For ages this imposing word led a harmless existence meaning no more than a 'place for which a person or thing is bound' (*COD*). About forty years ago there was a film called *Destination Moon*, but the word went on as before until some time in the 1980s. Then somebody in the ever-growing tourism industry saw the need for a new or newish expression meaning a 'place you travelled to for pleasure', and *destination* stood ready. In no time the Sunday papers were full of travel destinations and tourist destinations and, soon enough, just destinations, the noun alone coming to stand for a place you went to on a trip or on holiday or, nowadays, for a break. Useful word that, *break*, by the way, implying what must often be falsely that the holiday-maker is actually snatching a hard-earned and brief respite between two bouts of taxing, responsible work or even toil.

To resume: *destination* has arrived. The word retains its pompous railway-guide feel, but it is quite long and sonorous and does seem to dignify bloody awful places like Blackpool and Acapulco. Nevertheless it exemplifies a trend worth resisting.

Dialect or language?

Dialect is a difficult word to define, not least in that, unlike *language*, it may be taken as derogatory by a speaker of the dialect in question. Is Scotch (or Scottish, or Scots) a dialect of English spoken in (parts of) Scotland or a language in its own right? Is Welsh a language or a variety of Gaelic or Celtic along with other varieties like Breton and Manx? Or Catalan and Basque, is either or both or neither a dialect of Spanish? Is Romansh, variously spelt and sometimes known as Ladin, a language or a dialect? Is Norwegian a national language or a dialect of Danish? Is Flemish roughly the same as Dutch, or a dialect of Dutch, or a national language? And how are Mexican and other Latin-American forms of Spanish related to metropolitan and/or Castilian Spanish? And what about, say, the Indian or Red Indian or Amerindian or native American languages?

The answers to these questions would in practice largely

depend on who is answering them. I am thinking not only for instance of personal history and ancestry and national and/or regional pride, but also of what the respondent might know of language(s) and dialect(s) outside direct experience. There would obviously be much consensus on such matters as whether German and Dutch are related to each other, and some people who speak neither language would be able to pick out obviously cognate forms in words for *mother*, *father*, etc. But no general consensus or overall definition of terms like *dialect* and *language* can be made to emerge. Nor is expert knowledge helpful in this way. It is rightly too particular, too partial, too local, in a word too expert to illuminate large, vague questions.

I am interested in language and therefore in linguistic matters, but I am not and never have been an expert on any branch of them. I suppose I came nearest to being one when I was studying Latin and Greek at school. Since then my reading has been unorganised and probably superficial, with a few approaches to learning something when I found myself alongside the Welsh and their language in the 1950s. My first father-in-law knew some Romansh. My first novel was translated into Catalan early on, before achieving Spanish or French. Things like that.

As an anecdotal footnote, one that illustrates the distance between the amateur and the professional, I will recount my exchange a few years ago with a real linguist or linguistician. The talk (heavens knows how) had moved to similarities between languages and families of languages. I mentioned those of the Finno-Ugrian group spoken by communities to the east of those of the Indo-European group, the main representatives being Finnish and Hungarian. As far as I remember I passed over offshoots like Olonetsian and the Ob-Ugrian twosome. The philologist signified that I had acceptably described the relevant position in those parts.

'So Finnish and Hungarian are related,' I said.

'Finnish, Estonian and others on the one side, chiefly Hungarian on the other.'

'How closely are the main two related?'

'Oh, very closely indeed.' The man was not joking.

'Really. How closely is that?'

'Oh, as English and Greek, for instance.'

'Fascinating,' I said.

On the other hand, when a linguistician tells you that there were once dozens of entirely unrelated language-families in North America, you may take it that they were in truth entirely unrelated.

Dialogue

In the past, talks or discussions on important subjects were considered to be satisfactorily described as *talks* or *discussions*. Nowadays the two sides in a dispute, for instance, are apt to be engaged in (wait for it) a *meaningful dialogue*. The first element of this phrase is an absurdity, since no dialogue is meaningless, and the second illiterate, since any reasonable number can take part in dialogue or a dialogue. More charitably, perhaps, it can be said that we sympathise with the wish to assure reader or hearer that *these* talks or discussions are designed to get somewhere, not just to fill in time, but we have seen often enough what becomes of even well-formulated intentions. And anyway the whole meaningful-dialogue expression looks and sounds unbearably pompous. Nevertheless one would not wish to be deprived of a phrase that so unerringly points out its user as a humourless ninny.

Dictionary

It used to be said, probably with much truth, that every literate household possessed a Bible and a copy of *Pilgrim's Progress*. During the nineteenth century, the works of Shake-

speare and of Dickens would often have added themselves
to these and, towards its end, an English dictionary, one of
the smaller ones.

Nowadays, the shelf where these volumes would once
have stood has been replaced by a longer one bearing video
recordings. In particular, the habit of owning and often
consulting a dictionary has largely died out among the
general public. This decline has gone hand in hand with
the disappearance of Latin, a language and a literature in
the pursuance of which the reader and occasional writer is
perpetually looking things up. Even those who make a
living out of words, like journalists, clearly own no dictionary or, if they do, would no more think of ever consulting
it than the Domesday Book.

Somebody of my sort of age and taste is bound to experience a series of unpleasant little surprises here. Two such
turned up the other day in the correspondence columns of
what would undoubtedly call itself a quality newspaper.
Both were mild complaints, one that the phrase 'the Greek
Calends' was left unglossed in a recent issue, the other that
a few not very hard-looking words of French had not been
translated. When I had stopped screaming with rage I
checked that the Greek Calends were indeed glossed in the
smallest of my dictionaries. I have not much French but
enough, it was soon clear, to deal with the French phrase
objected to, perhaps actually recognised it. By now I had
nearly calmed down, not quite, though, because how dare
two grown-up people not penetrate such mysteries for themselves instead of advertising their ignorance? Easily enough
is the answer, in an era when even quite inquiring types
have got out of the habit of looking things up.

Didacticism

One of the funniest articles in *MEU* is to be found under this head; Fowler likes nothing better than seeing off linguistic prigs and pedants. Before getting down to it here he notes didacticism as a characteristically male vice. (Agreed.) His two chief examples, *suttee*, referring to the former Hindu custom requiring a widow to immolate herself on her husband's funeral pyre, and the *Caliph* of Baghdad from the Arabian Nights, are doubtless not as immediately familiar as they once were, but both are just right for their purpose and recognisable enough. Fowler duly writes:

> The Anglo-Indian [of British birth with first-hand knowledge of India] who has discovered that the suttee he read of as a boy is called *sati* by those who know it best is not content to keep so important a piece of knowledge to himself; he must have the rest of us call it *sati* like ... himself; at any rate, he will give the rest of us a chance of mending our ignorant ways by printing nothing but *sati* and forcing us to guess what word known to us it may stand for.

And straight after that:

> The orientalist whose histories have made familiar with the *Khalif* is determined to rid us of the delusion ... that there ever was such a being as our old friend the Caliph ... The one truth is ... that *Khalif* has a greater resemblance to Arabic than *Caliph*; is that of any use to anyone who does not know it already? ... English is ... entitled to give what form it chooses to foreign words that it has occasion to use ... [or] why do we say *Germany* and *Athens* ... instead of *Deutschland* and the rest?

He says elsewhere:

> Pride of knowledge is a very unamiable characteristic, and the display of it should be sedulously avoided ... [as in the case of] *amuck* [didactically *amok*], *different to* [forbidden by didacticism], *journal* [which pedantry would confine to meaning a daily paper only, because one of its sources, the Old French word *jurnal*, seems to have meant *daily*], *shamefaced* [instead of historically correct *shamefast*], etc.

As so often with Fowler, his verdict was to have meant an end of the matter. But we all know that *amok* has driven out *amuck*, that *different to* is still thought to be a solecism, and above all that that right of the English language, as of any other, to devise its own forms for foreign names is under constant erosion. *Peking* was an English word for centuries before it was suddenly replaced by *Beijing*, however you pronounce it; *Ceylon* has notoriously been replaced by *Sri Lanka*; *Lyons* has reverted to *Lyon* (Lee-on(g)) and *Marseilles* (pronounced Marsails) to *Marseille* (MarSAY, often with an attempt at the French uvular trill in the middle); *Seville* and *Genoa* have come a step nearer being pronounced in the native fashion. What about Brussels and *Brussels*? Ah, that I predict will go on as before. The British/English form conveniently steers between *Bruxelles* and *Brüssel*, the Walloon and Flemish versions of the name of the Belgian capital.

Dilemma

This is a very precise and was once a very useful word meaning 'a position that leaves only a choice between two equally unwelcome possibilities'. Somebody in such a position was often said to be 'on the horns of a dilemma'; the

49

word was narrow and clear. Unfortunately it has ceased to be either and for many years has been resorted to by journalists and others on the look-out for a posh-appearing synonym for 'difficulty, quandary'. This perversion has made *dilemma* unusable by careful writers.

Dimension

At one time this furnished a relatively precise term of literary criticism. A dimension, then pronounced with a long I in the first syllable, was one of three observable in solid bodies, viz. length, breadth and depth, and certain characters in fiction were said to be two-dimensional, like say Parson Adams, or three-dimensional, like say Leopold Bloom. However deftly executed, the two-dimensional character was felt and perhaps said to want a third dimension, to lack depth or whatever was necessary to furnish a fully realised portrayal.

So matters rested for a time, perhaps rather unadventurously. Then about ten years ago and quite suddenly, limited characters in novels and plays began to be complained of as one-dimensional. I thought at first that critics and others were setting out to reduce such characters to mathematical lines, the only possible constructs in a single dimension. This seemed incomprehensible until it dawned on me that of course *dimension* was now pronounced in transatlantic fashion with a short I in the first syllable and had become no more than an additional vague, shoddy, tatty but fashionable synonym for *aspect* or *view* or *side* or *feature* or *characteristic* or what-have-you. A one-dimensional character thus lacked depth. Really?

Disappearance of Latin

My own career is a good example of many things, but none more than in my experience of the language and the literature of Ancient Rome. Like millions of my fellows, I was brought up in the 1930s to study Latin. When I was seventeen I switched to English, which nevertheless meant that I continued to study the classics, though less inflexibly than before. When I secured an award in English and went up to Oxford in 1941 I had the advantage of a largely classical training, for all that it seldom felt like any sort of advantage at the time.

The foregoing is a mere exordium in that I have no intention of going on to say that to have studied Latin is in itself somehow good for you or for your English style. It is not that a knowledge of Latin protects anybody from making mistakes about the meaning of English words, because the meanings of words are not fixed, they change in and after their move from one language to another. It is true that *defendo* means 'I defend,' but a muscle is not a little mouse, which etymologically it is, nor is a pencil what its origins declare it to be, a doubly small penis. Neither is it the case that, as schoolmasters are supposed to have thought or said at one time, one was helped to think by mastering that language, as if it were a course of mental gymnastics. Nevertheless the student of Latin, as of any considerable dead language, must constantly be trying to choose the right word to give the meaning of a Latin expression in English or an English expression in Latin. And if the writing of English generally is in decline, as many would say it is, we may be tempted to say that people no longer try to choose the right word as they once did. They often got it wrong, but they tried. Do they now?

Something like the foregoing sketch might be developed to accompany an analysis of English poetry as written over the last fifty years or so. If this is seen as having become not only less formally organised but less exact in its expression, then the loss of Latin has surely had a hand in the matter somewhere. Again, I do not simply mean that an acquaintance with Propertius or Catullus in the original is beneficial to any sort of poet, though I think I do think so, but just as simply that translation into and out of Latin verse calls for exactness, and that that quality is demanded in the writing of poetry as nowhere else. Exactness, by the way, is to be understood as applying to more than denotation: a word or phrase must be suitable to its context, so that a dialectal or slang term, for instance, is on the whole unlikely to fit well into a passage of high seriousness – except for special effect, as teachers used to add.

The chances are that no particular virtue attaches to Latin as a language, although its role in our culture is unique and uniquely important. Any dead language will do as the kind of trainer I mean, such as Ancient Greek or, were it copious enough and intelligible, Etruscan. But deadness is necessary. A living language is by definition unfixed, in a state of continuous development and change, taking up, adapting and often dropping dialecticisms, provincialisms, technical terms, slang of all sorts, foreign expressions and more. It has no choice but to be useless as any sort of example.

The preceding paragraphs are no doubt speculative. What follows is all too manifest. Not just Latin itself has disappeared but in many cases any certain knowledge of what it was. A phrase like *mutatis mutandis*, apart from being offensively unintelligible to almost every British person, will be taken as a bit of Italian or French or (it's tempting to add) Choctaw rather than Latin. You come across it on old gravestones and monks used to sing it, or in it. The rest is silence. Latin is not only dead but cancelled.

When I was at school, the so-called New Pronunciation of Latin had come into use, though some elderly teachers now and then slipped back into the Old. The NP aimed at speaking Latin as the Romans had spoken it, the OP spoke Latin words as if they were English. So, for instance, the Latin phrase just quoted would come out as *mootahteece mootundeece* in NP, as *mewtehtice mewtandice* in OP. That great Latinist and headmaster, F.R. Dale, always insisted that NP was called for when you were speaking Latin and OP for English; after all it was Victoria not Wicktohria Station and a vacuum not a wahkuoom cleaner. It seemed logical as well as clear.

As Latin began to be less studied in schools, so, perhaps oddly, did people lose their memory of OP versions and more and more use NP, or something like it. By 1970 or so that process was complete. Today, when dealing with phrases that have entered the English language, like *prima facie* and *a priori*, non-Latinists say *preema fackiay* and *ah preeoree* if they use them at all, and whether or not they muddle them and their meanings up together as they are, perhaps more often than Latinists, apt to do. That much larger number of Latin phrases that have never entered our language or only done so among specialised speakers, like *sine die* or *in statu pupillari*, keep their OP integrity as *siney die-ee* among lawyers and *in staychoo pewpillairigh* in academe and seldom get used elsewhere.

Well, there we are, and nobody is much worse off in any obvious way. We may be more noticeably worse off in the pronunciation of some ordinary English words. I suggest that this has been affected by a haziness about foreign origins resulting from the loss of Latin both as a language and as a concept. Quite recently I heard over the air a trade-union boss talk of a *vayto* (veto) and a Cabinet minister of a *vayicle* (vehicle), both nouns vaguely foreign-looking words on the page. Longer ago I and others heard *dayity* (deity) and *spontanaity* for the first time. And here perhaps is the place to mention the *Tay Dayum* and countless other NP-ings of once deeply entrenched OP words and phrases.

Unfortunately as it may well be, the world has moved

on in the last fifty years. Once upon a time you might have been understood if you had mentioned Rossini's *Staybat Mayter* (Stabat Mater) or the *Die-ease Eye-ree* (Dies Irae), but this is much less likely today. Two maxims are worth recalling: The prime object of speech is to convey meaning, not to be right in any other sense; and Consistency is usually impossible. Nevertheless . . . Well, nevertheless the demise and departure of Latin are constantly to be regretted, at least.

This demise and departure, in this country, have not been total; life might be easier in some respects if they had. What might possibly be called living mummifications of a few bits of it are still to be found in ordinary written English, often of an old-fashioned sort and usually abbreviated. (I exclude here those specialised types of discourse like those involving lawyers and academics, as noted.) Anybody who may be offended by having familiar meanings spelt out should instead feel good at being one of a select few. Old Pronunciation used except where noted.

alias originally meant 'at another time'. Then it became a handy short noun meaning 'a name one is called by on special occasions, mainly disreputable', as in 'On the job his alias was Bloggs,' 'When having a bit on the side he used his mother's maiden name as an alias.' Then it got too hard to understand and was pushed out by the dull *aka* (pronounced *eh-kay-eh*), 'also known as'.

alibi originally meant 'somewhere else'. Then it became a handy short noun meaning 'ground for pleading one was elsewhere when a deed was done', as in 'his brother gave him a satisfactory alibi.' Then it came to mean merely 'excuse' and is now obsolete in any sense.

cf. Abbreviation for *confer*, the Latin not the English word. Means 'compare'. Being driven out by *cp* − 'compare'.

D.V. Abbreviation for '*Deo Volente*', 'God willing', 'if all goes well'.

e.g. Abbreviation for *exempli gratia*, 'for [the sake of an] example'. Often confused with *i.e.*

etc. Abbreviation for *et cetera*, 'and [the] other things'. Sometimes used in defiance of Latinity instead of *et al.*, in full *et alii*, 'and [the] other people'.

et seq. Abbreviation for *et sequentia*, 'and [the] following things', in practice usually pages. Being driven out by *and foll.*

ib[*id*] Abbreviation for *ib*[*idem*], 'in the same book, chapter, passage' etc. Very useful.

i.e. Abbreviation for *id est*, 'that is'. Often confused with *e.g.*

op. cit. Abbreviation for *opus citatum*, 'the work quoted'.

pace. An awkward word, to be avoided in one's own writings. *Pace tua* means 'by your leave', *pace* Bloggs means 'if Bloggs will give me leave' to say something he will very likely disagree with. So you might write, '*Pace* many true patriots, our country's interests will not be well served by any form of European union.' But you will risk incomprehension or misunderstanding. Pronounced, if ever, *pachay*, as if it were an Italian word. Recast your sentence.

passim. Literally 'in a scattered fashion' but is used to mean 'in every part' of author or work mentioned, as in 'found in Homer [or the *Iliad* etc.] *passim.*'

Q.E.D. Quod erat demonstrandum, 'which was to be proved or shown'. Found at the end of theorems and formerly in smart talk.

R.I.P. comes in a little oddly here, but had better come in somewhere. For *requiescat in pace*, 'may he/she rest in peace'. Often thought wrongly but harmlessly, indeed quite helpfully, to stand for 'rest in peace'.

sic means literally 'so', but is 'appended in brackets after a word or expression in a quoted passage as guarantee that it is quoted exactly, though its incorrectness or absurdity suggest that it was not' – from definition in 5th edn. of *COD*. Good going to get all that said in three letters. My stylistic advice is to be very sparing with the word as a way of noting supposed absurdities, as in, say, 'the sergeant called for volunteers [*sic*].' It is too harsh for such an unimportant context. But useful in the margin of typescripts as a warning to the printer to follow copy.

viz. is shortened from *videre licet*, 'one may see'. Usually spoken as *namely* and used as in, say, 'The Grand Fleet comprised all manner of vessels, *viz.* carriers, heavy cruisers, light cruisers, corvettes, sloops . . .' But 'namely' will do as well here and in all other contexts I can think of.

Disinterested

The most famous and ancient of all misuses and not for that reason any less a case of ignorant bullshit. Nowadays perhaps this depraved form is responding to decades of denigration and starting to become less popular than its virtuous cousin, 'uninterested'. For all that, by a process not altogether unique, the misuse has acquired a shade of meaning of its own. Thus a schoolboy who is *uninterested* in the lesson will merely be sunk in mindless apathy and gloom, whereas his *disinterested* classmate will be pulling faces and launching paper aeroplanes, actively expressing boredom. Compare FORTUITOUS.

E

Eke out

This once useful and individual phrase has now, in familiar style, been relegated to the status of a dozen near-synonyms. Nowadays you eke out a subsistence by scratching and scrimping, watching the pennies, carrying on somehow, struggling along, just keeping your head above water, living from hand to mouth, contriving to keep body and soul together, and so on. But in the days when words meant what they said you eked out your dull diet with nasturtium leaves, or eked out your defective income (inadequate legacy, pension, etc.) with other payments. *Eke*, then, was an archaic adverb meaning *also* and the verbal expression remembered that. So in practice you *eked out* the small allowance from your firm or under your father's will with consultancy fees or the proceeds of domestic work. The objection to slipshod language is not so much its remissness, though there is that, as its effective elimination of useful expressions. As things now are, to refer to what used to be *eking out* you have to go into tedious Latin polysyllables about supplementing sources of resources.

Elevator

Everybody knows that this is a 'needless' American variant for British *lift*. No doubt in a different and better world *elevator* would have remained a needless and so nonexistent such variant, but in the USA in the nineteenth century and later there were swarming immigrants who knew little or no English and to some of whom an obviously Latin-based polysyllable with a restricted meaning might have been more quickly grasped than a monosyllable easily missed or confused, to say nothing of the possible indecent overtones of *lift* (see SUCKING PIG) nor of any supposed preference for long words. It seems fair to add that, as a name for a passenger hoist, *elevator* has made no headway in the UK, and that it seems a bit much to scold Americans for using an Americanism in America.

Emulate

Like any other Latinate pedant, I used to pronounce this word with a long E at the beginning, until corrected the other day by a theatrical person. Anyway, I was not far out in mentally connecting the word with the Latin *aemulari*, 'to rival', however little that may seem to matter. The prime meaning of *emulate* is 'try to equal or surpass', so it is not what some people perhaps take it for, a recherché synonym for *imitate*. Such people show their ignorance by constantly writing things like 'he resolved to try to emulate Swift.' Trying to try to equal is a rarefied concept, more so, I cannot help thinking, than the writer intended. The word is still usable with caution.

England

(For 'En-gland' see SPLITTING WORDS.) While this word and its derivations are still usable, can we not all agree on their pronunciation, such that the first syllable rhymes with 'sting' and does not make the sound *eng* as spelt, a noise that would be unique in the language? To follow spelling in this case has never been frequent, and the usage has been on the verge of dying out for a long time, but it is still occasionally to be heard from broadcasters and others. Surely it deserves to be totally forgotten.

The spelling-pronunciation is unhistorical as well as unnecessary and pedantic. In early days, that first vowel was represented by an Old English letter that gave the short A to be found in Modern English words like *hat*: compare the *Anglo* in 'Anglo-Saxon'. But from early medieval times onwards that first syllable had a short I in it, as it has today and as is testified by foreign versions of the word *English*. The Portuguese *Inglês*, with its 'hushed' final consonant, is almost as close to *English* as could be hoped for.

The language group that most stands out against this practice is the Germanic. In German itself the words for *England* and *English* begin with a short E pronounced very like the English equivalent. In fact the German word *Englisch* is about as close to the unhistorical etc. version of the English word as could be wished. If you want to pronounce the name of our nationality and language as a German would, I cannot stop you. But I will do my level best.

England are

Grammatical parvenus get a lot of fun out of demonstrating they have learnt to count up to two by pouncing on plural subjects with singular verbs and vice versa. One favourite object of their uninstructed scorn is things like the headline ENGLAND FACE DEFEAT (at cricket, say). 'How can a singular noun like *England* take a plural verb like *face*?' they ask rhetorically. But ENGLAND FACES DEFEAT (in war?) means something quite different. Anybody with a tittle of wit knows that country-plus-plural refers to a sporting event or something similar. This is precisely what the verb is doing in the plural. It shows that a number of individuals, a team, is referred to, not one thing, a country.

Enormity, enormous

Centuries ago these two words must already have begun to drift apart and now are as separate as their respective meanings, viz. great wickedness (noun) and very large (adjective). When Milton wrote of Nature in Paradise pouring forth 'enormous bliss' he was making a learned pun, giving a reminder of the Latin roots (*ex-* or *e-* = out of, *norma* = norm, the ordinary) while testifying to the sheer size or quantity of the bliss. But when Eliot (TS) wrote of 'the *enormity* of man's ignorance' he was just getting it wrong: by rights he should have written *enormousness*. A fine example of English style he was, with his 'juvescence of the year' when he should probably have written *juvenescence*, though that might have been wrong too for his purposes.

Such hiccups aside, however, *enormity* and *enormous* continue on their way and are quite safe to use while they keep their stations as outlined above.

Ere

I mention this dead and unlamented word only to note that its ghost is sometimes raised by jocular chaps who affect phrases like 'ere long' and 'ere now'. I have two messages for such chaps: one is unprintable, the other goes, If you must write this shred of battered facetiousness, for Christ's sake get it right. The word is *ere*, not *e'er*.

Especial(ly), special(ly)

These words are obviously related and share their origin in the Latin *species*. Fowler begins his article on them by saying:

> The characteristic sense of the longer adjective and adverb is pre-eminence or the particular as opposed to the ordinary, that of the others being limitation or the particular as opposed to the general.

This is well observed and expressed, as one might have known, and would meet wide assent, but it is not calculated to function as a handy guide to anyone who might want to be told which is correct in which circumstances. Let me try.

The 'tendency' that Fowler went on to note, for the adjective *especial* to disappear and its place to be taken by *special*, has now become an accomplished fact. Nobody now talks or writes about *my especial friend* or *my especial subject*, though we should remember that past usages of this kind are not necessarily affected or unnatural. *Special* will now do all the jobs *especial* used to do as well as those it used to do itself.

The adverb *especially* remains and will probably continue. It survives in contexts where something like *in particular* or *even more so* is meant, as for example:

> This was meant for all town-dwellers, *especially* those in the south of England.
> I took this as directed against my family in general and *especially* myself.

Speciality is to be preferred to *specialty*, which is either a legal term or an Americanism meaning the same as *speciality*.

It may just be worth trying to remember that *special* was and perhaps still is an adjective connoting counterespionage or other security involvement, as Special Branch, Special Services, Special Wireless.

Exciting

An exciting film used to be so called because of the shoot-ups, car-chases, etc. it contained; now a film is said to be exciting if it contains what are thought to be innovations in technique, setting, etc. In fact, a person from the quite recent past might expect whole populations to be in a state of nervous collapse, so exhausted must they be by ceaseless exciting dishes, exciting drinks, exciting styles of dress or adornment, exciting new offers, exciting suggestions about anything and everything in their lives. A comparable person of our day, however, has learnt that *exciting* is just another advertiser's word used of a product that with luck will catch people's fancy and, in sober language, turn out to be mildly interesting or pleasurable.

Having ridiculed what was then a newish absurdity in a novel of 1968, I had started to hope that *exciting* in this sense had passed its sell-by date (to use another shopworn novelty). No such luck. This very morning I get a letter from somebody calling herself a Customer Service Manager informing me that 'so far, this has been an exciting year for Cable London customers.' I doubt whether the two excitement-engendering events quoted, the launching of a new Travel Channel in April and of Sky Sports 2 in August, are quite enough to do the whole job between them, though perhaps the advent of Channel One ('the brand new news and entertainment channel for Londoners') which will be 'hitting' my screen in early December, will shed a sort of retrospective fever of excitement over the whole of 1994.

This is perhaps as good a place as any to recall one of the sayings of the late Philip Larkin, dating from the 1950s, I think. 'I can't see why there's all this fuss about the human race perhaps being wiped out in the near future. It certainly deserves to be.'

Excuse me butting in

(A) Excuse me butting in, but there's a wasp on your collar.

(B) There are many questions to be asked about America's interest in the Caribbean, but the world awaits a reasoned explanation of the President's ordering an invasion of Santo Diabolo.

The two participle-like words, *butting* and *ordering*, are in fact verbal nouns or gerunds, and in strict grammar each should have a noun or pronoun in the possessive case attached to it, saying whose butting and whose ordering is being talked about here. Wasps on collars, however, might be felt not to go with strict grammar, and few actual people are likely to mention or even notice that strictly incorrect *me* instead of *my*, indeed to say *my* in (A) would be more likely to raise an eyebrow or two, if only in retrospect.

To speak plainly, the gerund is on the way out. Many writers would say that they feel an obligation to introduce a possessive in leisurely, formal sentences like (B), but are prepared to drop it, reluctantly or not, if they sense that what they write as a result is unnatural or stiff or awkward. It does seem as if they usually sense something like that.

People knew where they stood in the days when there was a firm rule about gerunds, familiar as these strange-sounding things then were from the study of Latin. One feels tempted to say that in an ideal world that rule would no doubt be kept, and the objection that we have to live in the real one is not a satisfactory answer. Whatever the merits of any rule, however, it serves no purpose if nobody obeys it. I suggest a practicable compromise as follows:

1. Do some work on learning to recognise gerunds. Remember they are verbal nouns, end in *-ing*, look like a participle but behave like a noun, the name of an action or state of being.
2. In real situations with real wasps, you will of course find you forget about any rule or the duty to keep it. But when writing you may wish not to affront such a rule. If you do, recast the sentence, as always.
3. When writing a (B)-type sentence, give the President his apostrophe-S unless it feels unnatural. If in doubt recast the sentence.
4. But in a (B)-type sentence where a pronoun is involved instead of a President, use the possessive of that pronoun. Sentences on the following model are thus recommended:

Instead of my [your, his, her, its, one's, our, their] opening the discussion with a formal statement, perhaps the chairman should ask for contributions from the floor.

Execute

I bring this word up not to protest about its being used with the new meaning 'put to death by law', nor to contend that by rights the sentence, not the criminal, is executed. That cause is well and truly lost, and the new meaning has for years been the main one. I mention *execute* only because till recently it was thought by the half-educated that it meant not merely to kill judicially but to do so by decapitation with axe, sword or guillotine, a historian's word for a historical thing. Now that historians have found something more relevant to teach than the removal of past monarchs and pretenders, this transitory and lesser sense has most likely passed into oblivion.

Expert

If asked, and quite possibly without being asked, an expert in the year 1800 might have told you the tale that Shotover Hill near Oxford got its name from an exploit of the legendary Little John, who is supposed to have once shot an arrow over it, no doubt for a bet. An expert of early Victorian times might well have said that that was 'unscientific' and that *Shotover* is a corrupt form of *Chateau Vert*, presumably an erection of Norman times now demolished. By 1900 if not before it was established that neither 'explanation' held water, that *Shotover* comes from two Old English words and that the name of the topographical feature is Hillhill Hill, or is so paraphrasable. Thanks a lot.

In the same sort of way, nobody believes any more that King Canute really expected the tide to retreat at his bidding, nor that he staged the show on purpose to demonstrate to his superstitious court that kings were not superhuman. So what was he really up to? The answer is full and clear: nobody knows. Oh, experts are agreed that he was actually called Cnut. Thanks another lot.

Twenty years ago or more I wrote a poem putting some of these points, but it was not much good. I threw in near the end the suggestion that experts consciously enjoy exploding attractive myths, which I no longer believe even if I believed it then. cf. OK, OKAY.

F

False unions

There is a tendency, not always deplorable in itself, to write or print as one word what used to be two, as in *underway*, *worthwhile*, *anyrate*, *daresay*, *percent*, *anymore*, *thankyou*, *onto* and others. Some of the others are deplorable in one place but above reproach elsewhere. So *come to lunch sometime* is deplorable, not only socially, but *a sometime* [i.e. former] academic is acceptable; *come to lunch just anytime* is also doubly deplorable, but in my view *anytime* scrapes by as a newish adjective in informal contexts, as *a popular anytime drink*.

Sometimes one has to write *all ready*, *any way*, *every one* and *in to* (*he came in to see me*), and an eye must be kept out for such cases.

But the vilest false union of all is *forever*, the prettified, sanitised version of a solemn, resounding phrase. Still not permissible with the frivolous meaning 'a lot of the time', as in *I'm forever blowing bubbles*. To be outlawed altogether.

cf. ALL RIGHT

Feminism in language

This is so notorious already, and such a joke, that I will offer only one comment. A sane feminist, and there must surely be such a creature, would presumably look forward to a perhaps far-off day when the feminist revolution is a

67

fact like the Russian one, when women are so fully the equals of men that feminist propaganda and other pressures have ceased to be needed. Until that day comes, of course, propaganda etc. will continue as usual, if not more so.

I have to confess that I, no doubt among others, have already begun to yield. Unable or unwilling to face the chore of perpetually remembering to write 'he or she' in appropriate contexts, I fall back on plural or passive constructions. If after a quick search these seem not to be available I recast the sentence. Why? Because I would rather be safe than sorry, and to find myself the occasion of some feminist outburst about unconscious (or conscious) chauvinism would make me very sorry indeed. Has that ever happened to me? Not yet, but we know well enough by now that all men are cowards, do we not?

Few

One might have thought that only a foreigner would confuse *few* with *a few*, paraphrasable as 'some but not many' and 'not many but some', but if so one would have been mistaken. A more frequent error involves the comparative *fewer*. This word can properly be used of countable entities like cabbages and kings. The word for a smaller quantity of something uncountable, like sugar and spice, is *less*. The error I refer to is the use of *less* when *fewer* is meant; correctly, we speak or write of *less* sugar but *fewer* cabbages. In ordinary conversation, some people perhaps feel that *less* is a more informal word than *fewer* and talk about *less* cabbages. This is forgivable if you like the people.

Figurative

This word used to mean 'metaphorical, not literal', and no
doubt still does in some contexts, for example those involving language, but in others, for example those involving
pictorial art, it has come to mean something not far off the
opposite of that. A *figurative* painting is in a style that shows
human and other figures in a recognisable form, and so is
nearer 'literal' than 'metaphorical'. Well, something associated with sanity is welcome back under almost any name.

Fine toothcomb

The kind of would-be grammarian who disdains locutions
like *England face defeat* is also apt to cackle gleefully at *fine
toothcomb/tooth-comb*, alleging that a *fine-tooth comb* is meant.
Whatever a crime reporter may write imaginatively about a
murder investigation, detailed inquiries, etc., perhaps there
never was such a thing as a tooth-comb, fine or not.

But there was, and still is according to the 1988 *COD*,
which precedes its own *tooth-comb* entry with the sign indicating a British usage and continues:

> (with fine close-set teeth; properly FINE[2] *toothcomb*, taken
> as *fine tooth-comb*)

Not so taken by me, and as regards *properly* the case is not
proven. As long ago as before the last war you could ask
for and buy over a shop counter something called a tooth-
comb, the sort that as well as fine teeth had an inches-long
spike at one end. No doubt you could have productively
asked for a fine or finer or less fine tooth-comb. Did the
COD editors know that? Or did they just fall in behind
the would-be grammarian's explanation? Not the second,
quite likely, but at least just as quite likely not the first

either. And when you edit a dictionary you have to be as certain as you can get.

Fivepence

This is virtually a non-existent word for a perhaps sufficiently existent thing, the sum of five pence in our new (adopted 1971) currency. The fact that decimal coinage has never caught on or been accepted here is quite sufficiently demonstrated by the equally hard fact that the sum mentioned has never been called *fivepence* but always 'five pee'; if the coin is meant it is called a 'five-pee piece', never a 'shilling', which is now a dead word in the UK. Similarly with 10p and the others. The others? The smaller denominations are seen less and less as inflation renders them obsolete. Fowler got it wrong for once.

Forensic

Until almost the other day it might have been worth averring that originally this word meant nothing more than 'of courts of law' and so, for instance, 'forensic evidence' meant nothing more than 'evidence offered in a court of law', like much evidence worthy of the name. But now *forensic* means erudite, sophisticated, concerned with things like fingerprints, bloodstains and other stuff criminological science may be able to draw evidence from, and *a forensic squad* no longer brings thoughts of a gang of policemen routinely engaged in the detection of crime but of a highly trained team of experts equipped with the latest in deductive apparatus and skills, of technicians. The origin of the word has been effectively forgotten so thoroughly that dreams of restoring the old meaning are vain even if the goal were desirable. Should then the righteous among us use *forensic* in its new meaning, as a distinct synonym of *technical*? No, is my vote. Say *technical* and forget that *tekhne* itself once meant *art*.

Fortnight

An obsolete term with its roots in Old English meaning a period of two weeks and used in phrases like *a fortnight today* to mean two weeks after today. The word has been replaced by the more regular *two weeks*, which is less idiomatic and duller but as always gives everybody one less word to remember and is at any rate American.

Fortuitous

Although Fowler was denouncing it back in 1926, the misuse of *fortuitous* has only become noticeable in the last decade or so. The word originally meant nothing more than 'owing to [pure] chance', as in, say, 'their meeting in the fish-shop was altogether fortuitous.' Recently, the word has come to mean something more like 'fortunate, by a lucky chance', as it might be in 'their meeting was most fortuitous, in that it led directly to their long and happy association.' In fact *fortuitous* now supplies the evident need for a single word with that meaning. Such a need may not be very compelling, but the more recent usage is serviceable and needful enough to suggest that such newcomers should not be shot out of hand. For after all, there are plenty of near-enough synonyms for *fortuitous* in the old sense, for instance 'chance' (adjective) as in 'chance meeting'.

Four-letter words

I am concerned here with words rather than ideas, although I know well enough that there is a connection between the two. So if I think present-day writers make more fuss about physical sex than I care to do, or describe it in more detail than I find comfortable, that difference must await full treatment elsewhere. Suffice it for the moment to notice that the change in what may be said has gone closely with how it may be said.

Both these things, all these things, have changed a certain amount since I wrote my first novel, *Lucky Jim*, more than forty years ago. No doubt with no more intention than to be friendly, to make intelligible the character of the hero, Jim Dixon, more recent critics have described him as a 'womanising' young man. Dixon could have wished no more flattering label for himself, but in fact his womanising, what there is of it, is virtually limited to his imagination. All he actually does, briefly set out, is throw some sort of physical pass at one girl and lay his hands on the clothed breast of another – the sort of 'womanising' that a modern hero would outdo in an opening paragraph. Incidentally I was conscious of no unnatural restriction on me at the time or later.

By 1955 the world had moved on. In my second novel the hero is stated, not shown, to go to bed with a female not his wife, and at another point a minor character is made to say of another, 'I feel sorry for that poor bugger.' My publisher, Victor Gollancz, telephoned to warn me that if I insisted on that six-letter word I might lose the 2000 (I think) copies I would otherwise dispose of to (I think) Boots' Booklovers' Library.

I considered briefly. 'What about "bloody fool"?' I asked.

'Perfectly acceptable,' said Victor.

So it proved. I have never felt entirely easy about the change, because 'bugger' in such a context does not count as swearing. It is, or was, a friendly synonym for 'chap' or 'customer' in South Wales, the setting of the story, whereas 'bloody fool' does or did count there as swearing as well as being inappropriate to speaker and situation. What a long time ago it all seems.

As the reader will know, the 1960s and their aftermath brought matters up to date. I have forgotten when I first said or made a character say *fuck* in print, but no one seemed to notice or care, any more than they did when my son Martin used the word several dozen times in one page in a novel published in 1978. Nor does it probably signify. All the same, I appear to have given myself a good chance to state and stress how much in the realm of bad language has changed over those years, not all of it for the better. Before, to utter or to write a swear-word, as they were called, counted as a small act of revolt, the breaking-out of a miniature Jolly Roger. Parents, grandparents, teachers, men in dog-collars, married men and subscribers to Boots' Booklovers' Library were dead against anything of the sort. So, for instance, when you let fall a swear-word in front of a contemporary you were among other things revealing yourself as a diminutive dissident and inviting your hearer to make a recognition signal. And when Philip Larkin used such words in letters to contemporaries he was not being 'misanthropic' or 'foul-mouthed' but being very mildly subversive and, like a good letter-writer, encouraging the recipient to feel he was a member of the same secret army as the sender. And what I was principally doing, by including in a letter to him a whole page of scurrility directed at our common publisher, was trying to entertain a friend. One would not even attempt such a thing these days, not by such means.

These days (to resume whence I have digressed) that particular conflict is over. Four-letter words are probably less in use conversationally than they were and, with the exception of one denoting the female parts, of less impact.

Their appearance on TV also seems reduced, now that people no longer utter them out of a boyish desire to show off. One taboo perhaps remains: as far as I know, nobody has yet said *fuck* to a senior member of the royal family. On the whole, the thinning-out of spoken ribaldry is a loss. An entire way of being funny, an entire range of humorous effects, has been impoverished, except probably on the lower deck of our society.

At first sight, the case with the printed four-letter word is different, though here I detect a similarly unwelcome drift towards serious aesthetic purpose. A bit of that can be seen in one of the last and least of the big *fuck*-novels, the winner of the 1994 Booker Prize. The doggedness with which its author keeps on trotting out the great word and its various derivatives already has something old-fashioned about it. Time for a change.

Naturally someone in my position has had to devise some rough rules governing the use of such words. My own set of rules I now put in writing for the first time. In what follows, *they* and *them* stand for what were once obscenities.

1. Use them sparingly and, as classicists used to say, for special effect only.
2. Even in low farce, never use any of them in its original or basic meaning unless perhaps to indicate that a character is some kind of pompous buffoon or other undesirable. Even straightforward excretory ones are tricky.
3. They may be used in dialogue, though remember rule 1. An attempt at humour will often justify their appearance. The power of making one male character say to another, 'She's a fucky *nuck* case' is not one to be lightly surrendered.
4. If in doubt, strike it out, taking 'it' here as one of them. (If one of them is not involved, my rule for myself is leave it in, especially first time round. I doubt if many writers get more ideas than they know what to do with.)

Fowler

Henry Watson Fowler (1858–1933), grammarian and lexicographer, is not quite the only writer on the English language mentioned by name in this book. Another is Frank George Fowler (1871–1918), his brother. The two collaborated on *The King's English* (1906) and *The Concise Oxford Dictionary* (first edn. 1911). Their literary partnership lasted from 1903 to 1918, latterly much interrupted by war service, which both brothers undertook though over military age, by illness and by the war itself. The elder was to write of the younger, 'In 1918 he died, aged forty-seven, of tuberculosis contracted during service with the B.E.F. in 1915–16.' H.W. greatly missed him, not least as a professional colleague and a collaborator, but for all that wrote and published his famous *Dictionary of Modern English Usage* in 1926.

This work, known for many years simply as *Modern English Usage*, is also known even more simply as *Fowler* in expressions like 'Fowler's view' and 'Fowler is unambiguous on the point.' However much H.W. Fowler might have resented this virtual exclusion of F.G. – and we are assured in its epistle dedicatory that F.G. shared in the planning stage of *MEU* – the outcome was inevitable in the circumstances.

Despite its age, the book remains uniquely indispensable to any serious survey of how we speak and write. Although it calls or called itself a dictionary, and contains many brief entries hardly going beyond the pronunciation or spelling of a word, 'much of it consists of short essays on various [pertinent topics], some with fancy titles that give no clue at all to their subject', as a reviser observed in 1965, and it is true that some of the writing needs the sort of close attention that its author deprecated as a requirement for ordinary reading. Nevertheless as a whole it has aged remarkably little over the years. Again and again the present-day reader will be willing to swear that such-and-such a usage has only the other day made its appearance, only to find that Fowler had already noticed it. This, together with the persistence of the 'superstition' against split infinitives, for instance, encourages the view that changes in the way we use language take a long time to happen. More briefly, it is never safe to assume that Fowler will have nothing to say on any given point.

The picture of him that emerges from his works is more informative than might be expected. Far from being any sort of conventional pedant he seems tolerant and humorous, clearly enjoying the duty of rebuking error which his task laid upon him, yet never merely destructive. He steers a rigorously unfanatical course between knowledge and common sense, and was saying something beyond both linguistics and politics when he writes in his *MEU* article on spelling (surely a subject that constitutes a potential trap for the pedagogic):

> . . . English had better be treated in the English way, and its spelling not be revolutionised but amended in detail . . . The well-known type theoretical-radical practical-conservative covers perhaps a majority of our nation, and its influence is as sound and sane in the sphere of spelling as elsewhere.

Nothing about H.W. Fowler is changed, though something is added, when account is taken of details of his life other than his volunteering to fight for his country at the age of fifty-six. He had started his professional career as a master at Sedbergh in Yorkshire, but resigned after seventeen years over a difference of opinion with his headmaster, Fowler taking what might be called a freethinking line. In 1908 he married 'a lady four years younger than himself' and enjoyed a happy life with her for over twenty years. He kept himself fit by refusing to employ servants and by going on runs and swims well into the winter. He was described by a former pupil of his at Sedburgh as 'a man of great fastidiousness, moral and intellectual'. In some respects he was an excellent example of a not uncommon type in nineteenth-century England, a muscular non-Christian who nevertheless learnt his values from the doctrine of that Church.

Modern English Usage is better than a worthy memorial to its author. It not only stands as the crown of his achievement but also it has gone on being continuously interesting, helpful and to the point in a way that no comparable production, if there is such a thing, has ever managed to do. Anything that might be got out of this book of mine will only come from my having had Fowler open beside it. It was once said that, despite any later developments, a canny Shakespearean scholar would know it was sound policy (as well as entertaining) to see first what Samuel Johnson had had to say on a given passage before turning to more recent commentators. The same and more besides should apply to Fowler in his own sphere. He and his work have never received the honour they deserve.

Frankenstein

1. Frankenstein (brilliantly named) is the eponymous character in a Gothic romance written by Mary Shelley in the early nineteenth century. He makes something like a human being from bits of dead bodies and gives the result life. The creature is fundamentally good, but after much ill treatment from humankind becomes the instrument of Frankenstein's destruction.
2. In the early twentieth century, when science and technology seemed to be expanding at a great rate, it was natural for writers to look for images of human invention over-

reaching itself. The Frankenstein myth was pressed into service, but in a simplified or garbled form whereby the name of Frankenstein became attached to the monster. Those who talked about the danger that humans would create a deadly Frankenstein were sternly and regularly rebuked for linguistic impropriety by such as Fowler.

3. After a time, whether as creator or monster, Frankenstein was no longer to be found in newspaper columns. Perhaps he had simply gone out of fashion. Or perhaps the whole question of how to refer to him had been made too difficult or cumbersome to handle. If the latter, it was something of a triumph for the sticklers.

French expressions

The rule I follow in talk is to use only such French expressions as have no reasonably exact and often-used equivalent in English. It is pointless and may be discourteous for one English-speaker to talk in French to another English-speaker outside the classroom, and something similar applies to whatever may be written and printed. So when I hold forth a female singer gets called that and not a *cantatrice*, and so on.

The pronunciation of a French word or words should, when the language of conversation is English, avoid any attempt at exact French pronunciation, which can hinder the flow of talk. At the same time, a speaker will not pronounce every French expression as if it were English. To do so is all right for some French words, like those in *tour de force*, which a sensible English-speaker will pronounce without any French sounds whatever. But many others would sound so non-English that some compromise seems called for, like *tant pis* or *aide-de-camp*, which are unintelligible as English noises. In the list that follows, which is shorter than Fowler's of eight or nine hundred, I have tried to keep everything to a minimum, very much including my signs for awkward sounds. Only expressions perhaps inaccessible to common sense are included. Menu French is omitted: consult the waiter. ** indicates an expression to be pronounced in as English a fashion as is reasonably possible; any attempt at a Frenchified pronunciation, except among the young and uninstructed, is to be regarded with grave suspicion. Throughout, be ready to make allowance for my accent, which in non-linguistic terms comes from south-eastern England, so for instance I don't pronounce the R at the end of *water* and in the middle of *Saturday*, and this is reflected here in my re-spellings of French words. The sound every English-speaker makes at the end of words like *china*, represented in phonetic alphabets by a lower-case E turned upside down, is here denoted by *uh*. French words are signified by italics: *aide-de-camp*, *amateur*. English words, or attempts to tell an English reader how I think he/she should pronounce a French word, are conveyed in roman: thus aid-duh-CON(G) and AM-a-tuh. Some clumsiness and ugliness result, but better so than obscurity.

aide-de-camp. Pronounce aid-duh-CON(G). Or just say and write A.D.C.
amateur. AM-a-tuh if non-professional is meant. If (archaic use) enthusiast or devotee is meant, a-ma-TUR.
apéritif. Ignore the accent and pronounce as English, stress on second syllable.
attaché. Suitcase is a-TATCH-y, diplomat is a-TASH-ay.
banquette. Bon-KETT.
belles-lettres. Bel-LETT-ruh.
blancmange. Bluh-MONJ.
blasé. BLAH-zay.
café. CAFE-ay. Caff-AY is for Americans. Also, humorously, for lowbrow eatery, caif, as in Finkel's caif.

canapé. CANnapay.

celeste. SillEST.

charlatan. SHARlatuhn.

chauffeur. SHOfuh. ShoFUR is for Americans and their imi-
tators. Old posh chaps once said SHUVvuh to rhyme with
'cover'; not any more.

connoisseur. ConnuhSUR.

coup d'état. Coo dayTAH.

coupon. **

débâcle. DAYbarkle. If you must.

dénouement. DayNOOmon(g).

détour. DAYtour.

distrait, distraite. DisTRAY, disTRAYT.

dossier. DOSSy-eh, three syllables.

élite. EllEAT.

en masse. On mass as in English.

esprit de corps. EssPREE duh COR.

faux pas. Foh PA.

fiancé, fiancée (if still in use). English pronunciation will no
longer do. So feeON(G)say for both.

garage. GARahzh. I know the word has been in English use
quite long enough for it to be pronounced in the English
way, to rhyme with marriage, but it seems I can't bring
myself to the point.

hors d'oeuvres. Aw DERV and no messing. Not an infallible
wanker-detector, but it can safely be said that few non-
wankers over the age of, say, twenty-one try to say the
words in any Frenchified way. If Fowler had been writing
now I very much doubt whether he would advise the
pronunciation orRdEU'vr(*e*) as he does in *MEU*.

idée fixe. EEday FEEKS.

je ne sais quoi. Zher ner say KWAH. Important to pronounce
in as English a way as possible.

liaison. **

liqueur. Lih-CURE. Any attempt to say lee-cur in a
Frenchified way is a useful wanker-detector.

macabre. MuhKAHbruh. Imagine yourself addressing a Scot called Macarbrough.

menu. ** I suppose there are people who try to pronounce this like a French word. Fowler seems to want us to say MENoo.

milord. MEElor. A Frenchification, hallowed by custom, of English 'my lord'. Avoid.

morale. MuhRAHL. Spelt with final E when meaning something like confidence.

naïf, naïve. Nah-EEV regardless of gender.

naiveté. Unnecessary in English.

nonchalant. **

penchant. PON(G)shon(g). Worth mentioning even if only because some Americans have been heard to say penshant, as if they thought it was an English word.

pension, meaning a boarding-house etc. PON(G)sion(g). Also not an English word despite some Americans.

pince-nez. PAN(G)snay. The only word for the thing, alas.

plaque. Say plahk rather than plack, which is hardly a word at all.

précis. PRAYsee.

recherché. RuhSHAIRshay. A good word for the quality.

reconnaissance. ** Note also *reconnoitre, -oiter,* **

restaurant. RESTront. For years I tried to anglicise this word as RESTrant, with -ant as 'pennant' etc., but eventually noticed that the familiar half-Frenchified form was more easily understood.

restaurateur. RestraTER. This man is a restorator, one who restores you and your energies, so, despite Roget, not spelt *restauranteur*.

revue. **

sabotage. SABBuhtahzh. One of those words like *garage* that resist attempts at full anglicisation.

sachet. SASHay. There is no reason not to say SASHit except that no one will understand you.

savoir faire. SAVwah fair. No English equivalent. 'Knack'

is not highbrow enough, and 'flair' is French likewise.

silhouette. ** Drop the H.

surveillance. **

terrain. **

timbre. TAMbruh, like an English word that ends in -borough.

trait. Trate.

turquoise. TURKwoize.

valet. VALLit.

wagon-lit. VAGGon(g)-lee.

From year to year

'He served in the Royal Pikestaffs from 1965 to 1980' or 'between 1965 and 1980' or '1965–1980', not a hybrid like 'from 1965–1980'.

Fulsome

This once useful word meant 'disgustingly excessive, cloying' as applied to compliments, apologies, etc.; Roget lists it between *gushing* and *stagy*. Undereducated persons, perhaps foggily supposing *fulsome* to be a posh form of *full* (from which it does partly descend), have in recent years taken to using it to mean 'ample' or possibly 'cordial'. Not to be used henceforth by careful writers.

G

Gay

The use of this word as an adjective or noun applied to a homosexual has attracted unusually prolonged execration. The 'new' meaning has been generally current for years. *Gay lib* had made the revised Roget by 1987 and the word itself was listed in the 1988 *COD* under sense 5 as a homosexual. There, however, the noun was entered in the 'slang' category, i.e. current among a restricted group. Surely, even in England today, the literate are not a restricted group, and anybody who can read must have long known what *gay* means. And yet in this very spring of 1995 some old curmudgeon is still frothing on about it in the public print and demanding the word 'back' for proper heterosexual use.

This is impossible. I admit I get as annoyed as anyone by being effectively debarred from quoting in public what Chesterton wrote at the beginning of his marvellous dedicatory poem to *The Man Who Was Thursday* (1908). Perhaps I can safely quote it now. The era referred to is the 1890s.

> A cloud was on the mind of men
>   And wailing went the weather,
> Yea, a sick cloud upon the soul
>   When we were boys together.
> Science announced nonentity
>   And art admired decay;
> The world was old and ended:
>   But you and I were gay.

The fact that such a stroke is impossible now should not blind us to the larger fact that, once a word is not only current but accepted willy-nilly in a meaning, no power on earth can throw it out. The slightest acquaintance with changes in a language, or a minimum of thought, will show this truth.

This time it is not wholly an unwelcome truth. The word *gay* is cheerful and hopeful, half a world away from the dismal clinical and punitive associations of *homosexual*. We lucky ones can afford to be generous with our much larger and richer vocabulary.

Gender

Many people would agree that this term would be best kept as what until the other day it exclusively was, a grammatical distinction between classes of noun and pronoun, together with the articles and adjectives appropriate to them. But then sex came into it as into much else in what we say and write, and the expression *a difference of sex*, for instance, was seen or thought to be chiefly concerned with sexual organs and their activities, chiefly enough to have to be specifically ruled out when these were not meant, and *gender* was an obvious way of signalling the fact. The discomfort that many people (the same sort of many people?) will have felt at this shift is not necessarily to be identified with that felt at most sorts of sexual intrusion. Part of it perhaps is a vague sense that something is being attacked or conceded, something to do with the recognition that the larger part of sexual behaviour is not physical but no less sexual for not being so, and the acceptance of *gender* as a non-grammatical term is to some degree a lowering of that flag.

Genteelism

This is Fowler's word for a very real and surviving thing, the synonym for a common or garden word that seems to some persons more elevated than that word, one 'that is thought to be less soiled by the lips of the common herd, less familiar, less plebeian . . .' like *ale* for *beer* (he rather ignorantly says; see ALE), *assist* for *help*, *endeavour* for *try*, etc. One sees what Fowler means all right, but some of his distinctions have become blurred by time, while others were perhaps shaky from the start. Thus a *carafe* (genteelism) was surely never indistinguishable from a *water-bottle* (described as the normal word for the thing); a *chiropodist* may in truth be no better than a *corn-cutter*, but he can hardly be expected to call himself that; *the military* is not at all the same as *soldiers*, as many civilians could testify; *mirror* is not, possibly never was, a genteelism for (normal word?) *looking-glass*. Contrariwise, one might, probably would, agree heartily that the normal verb *put* is far too often horribly supplanted by *place*, especially in the writings of journalists who think they are being suitably serious. And yet, again, one would surely prefer to say that the Queen Mother was *placed* behind the Queen in the Abbey than *put* behind her.

Not such an inflexibly organised character as he sometimes appears, Fowler has at least two more bites at this particular cherry, one under the heading of Formal Words, the other under Working and Stylish Words. In both cases he has good examples to quote – *donation* as a posh synonym for *gift*, *conceal* for *hide*, *obtain* for *get*, *seek* for *try* or *look for*, *feasible* for *possible*, *sufficient* for *enough*, etc. – and brisk general remarks to offer, such as:

What is to be deprecated is the notion that one can improve one's style by using stylish words . . . the writer who prefers . . . the stylish word for no better reason than

85

that he thinks it stylish, instead of improving his style, makes it stuffy, or pretentious, or incongruous,

and more weightily and positively,

Few things contribute more to vigour of style than a practical realisation that the *kuria onomata*, the sovereign or dominant or proper or vernacular or current names, are better than the formal words.

And yet, for the second or third time, the reader may object that to *peruse* is not just to *read* but to *read carefully*, that *catarrh* and *cold* are far from synonymous, that *violin* is not a 'stylish' word for the 'working' *fiddle*, but the standard word, the *kurion onoma*, for the instrument familiarly called a *fiddle* among musicians. The last objection may be a result of the passage of time; most others are not.

Calls for simplicity and unpretentiousness of style are perpetually welcome, but pressure for such virtues should not be elevated into any kind of rule. *Meal* or *lunch* or *snack* are undoubtedly better words in most circumstances than *collation* or *luncheon*. Nevertheless you can grab a *meal* or a quick *snack* in the kitchen, standing up if need be, of a couple of sandwiches, a spring onion and a can of beer (or ale); a *collation* involves sitting down to a number of courses and a *luncheon* a degree of formality, place cards, all that. The annoying truth is that almost every written word confronts the writer with a choice for which no rule will ever quite serve, and the price of a good style, like that of other desirable things, is eternal vigilance.

Germanisms

A mid-century American writer on the English language draws attention to the emergence of what he calls 'a construction deeply at variance with the genius' of that language, and quotes so-called '*easy-to-read books* for the children and *ready-to-bake* food for their mothers'. The same writer goes on to say:

> If we wish to protect ourselves from this new assault on our wits, we must begin by avoiding every form of easy compounding – e.g. *air-conscious* ... *career-* or *action-oriented, accident-prone, teenage-proof, budget-wise* ... It is a mistake to think that because everything is classifiable everything must be classified. And Germanisms in English are but clumsy attempts to stick labels on arbitrary groupings: *never-before-told incidents/a more-honored-in-the-breach situation/a let-the-devil-take-the-hindmost attitude,* to which we may add the multitude of definitions by *non-* (*nonfiction, nonviolent, nonreligious, noninsured*). Some of these last may be necessary but most of them only pretend to define.

Hereabouts the English reader may get the sense of having strayed into a domestic conflict, but there can be no doubt where the battle-lines are or which is the right side of them. Or that the enemy has powerful allies on this side of the pond.

Get, got

In my schooldays these were suspect words, not exactly erroneous in themselves but vulgar. *I'll get it* or *he's got it* were said to be expressions lazy/stupid people fell back on because they were too stupid/lazy to think of or to know genteel words like *obtain* or *possess*. Even today both *get* and *got* retain a whiff of informality, so they should be avoided in solemn contexts or when trying to impress an octogenarian.

Ancient anti-*got* feeling may have played a part in developing the American preference for *do-you-have* constructions over *have-you-got* ones. *Do-you-have* is spreading in this country perhaps in simple imitation, but perhaps also, unconsciously, to placate those choosy octogenarians. If it takes over altogether from *have-you-got* a shade of meaning will have been lost: *do you have* such-and-such means or meant 'do you normally have it?', whether *it* was indigestion or tinned cat-food, whereas *have you got* something implies 'at this moment'. But then no speaker was ever inhibited by thoughts of shades of meaning.

Golf

I bring up this word because some people still pronounce it *goff*, though most of them must be getting a bit long in the tooth by now. Any who do should switch to saying *golf* right away. To say *goff* nowadays is a form of didacticism, informing anybody who may be listening that this is how top people pronounce the word and also what the Scots, who invented the game, perhaps call it. Perhaps not; opinion is divided; whatever they may once have called it I doubt if many of them say the word differently from the rest of the GB population. I ask only that the O of golf should be of the short variety, as in *gob*, not the long, as in *go*.

Good-bye

Not only is the *good* in *good-bye* not the familiar English word *good*, but the *bye* is not what it may seem either. Every schoolboy used to know that *good-bye* was a contraction of *God be with you*, with *good* substituted for *God* probably on the analogy of leave-taking phrases like *goodnight*. Intermediate forms like Hamlet's *God be wi' ye* are recorded from the sixteenth to the eighteenth century, with the present form of the expression established some time in the latter.

The custom is to hyphenate *good-bye* and leave the others, *good night*, etc., unhyphenated. Incidentally *good evening* is a valediction only on television, and I have come across *good night* as a greeting only in the works of James Joyce.

Gorged-snake construction

This is an engaging but perhaps not strikingly apt American name for a journalistic trick that, like so many such, is not very objectionable in its place – in a newspaper report – but out of the question elsewhere. Any example is bound to be on the lengthy side, though I have made mine as short as I reasonably can.

> Briton Chris Mankiewitz, twenty-six, has been named to lead England's soccer squad against Ruritania next month.
>
> The Warsaw-born father-of-two said at his recently-rebuilt £150,000 Deptford home, 'My attractive blonde wife Samantha, twenty-four, and I are just over the moon with the news.'
>
> Success has come just in time for the whiskered former schoolboy hurdler champion star of Clapton Occident's injury-stricken midfielders.
>
> The much-photographed hat-trick specialist and avid sports-car driver, a familiar local figure in his blood-red Halberstadt D-VII . . .
>
> 'Looks like we're out of the woods for a bit,' laughed the tall dark sun-worshipper as he dubbined with his own hands the boots that . . .

Now I quite see that putting into some sort of logical order a couple of dozen facts about Briton Chris Mankiewitz would take longer than the supposed writer of the above could have afforded. Some such attempt, however, might have made it possible for the reader to remember a few of them on finishing the story. But then no newspaper story is meant to hold the attention longer than it takes to get from coming round after a snooze to the beginning of the first TV quiz show.

Greek remnants

Few people have ever learnt Greek or remember any. One phrase perhaps survives in ordinary talk: the *hoi polloi* = the (vulgar) majority. *Hoi* is itself a form of the word for 'the' but the accepted phrase, even among those who know this, is again 'the *hoi polloi*', pronounced hoy p'LOY. There are plenty of adequate synonyms in English.

Look up ahead of time any Greek (or Latin) name you may wish to use in talk, which will help you not to sound like an illiterate. As with ordinary words, actual Greek (or Latin) practice is no guide. The legendary founders of Rome, for instance, Romulus and Remus, are called Rommulus and Reemus in English, and it helps nobody to know or be told that in their day and in their language they were Rohmulus and Remmus. Nor would any normal person think of pronouncing the first syllable of *Socrates* to rhyme with *poh* or *poke*, only with *pock*. But the name *Pericles* does not rhyme with *clericals*, as somebody made it do on the radio the other day, and names in -*eus* end with the sound of the noun 'use', so we say *Perce-use*, not *Percy-us*. And a version of original accentuation is preserved, so the tendon that connects your heel and calf is still your *Achilles* tendon stressed on the second syllable no matter whether you know or care who Achilles was or why this particular tendon gets its name from him.

Remember to keep the *ch* hard in Greek-derived words like *triptych*, which is pronounced *triptick*, not *triptitch*. And *Graecist* or *Grecist* is pronounced like *grease-ist*, but quite soon the whole thing – Greek, Latin, Hebrew, Old English – will have blown over.

Gulf, the

This is how broadcasters and recent maps designate the place we all grew up calling the Persian Gulf, now robbed of its distinguishing adjective seemingly in order to placate, or not to offend, Iraq and perhaps other Gulf States. It strikes me as high time the Persian Gulf was given its historic name back. After all, the Gulf of Mexico is still so called whatever the USA and possibly other nationalities may think about it.

H

Letter H

1. After many years, people still need to be told to talk about *a historical novel*, not *an historical novel*, and *a hotel*, not *an hotel*, whereas mention of either *a* or *an hotelier* should be suppressed with bloodshed. The rule is that words beginning with an H only take *an* when they begin with a genuinely silent H, like *heir, honour, hour* and their derivatives. Words that merely look on paper as if they begin with a vowel sound, like *one, use* and *euphoria*, are preceded by *a*, not *an*, as you must know.
2. An uncombined H in the middle of a word, as in *philharmonic*, should not be sounded. (Unless it happens to begin a syllable, so you should pronounce the H in *philhellenism* should you ever find yourself using the word.) Words of foreign origin, however, like *bilharzia*, may require a sounded H, and thereafter let likelihood and common sense direct you. Woe betide anybody I catch pronouncing the name *Beethoven* with a separable H.

Hamstringed

The hamstring in human beings is one of five tendons at the back of the knee, and to *hamstring* a man is to cripple him by cutting this tendon. Metaphorically, one's enterprise or efforts can be *hamstrung*. Or is it, should it be, *hamstringed?* Yes, says Fowler. Take your choice, says the *COD*. No, say I: to use *hamstringed* in ordinary conversation is to run the risk of pedantry or, worse, of not being understood. No doubt *stringed* instruments are so called by musicians, but even in dictionaries it is a *string* bass and anxious people are all *strung* up, not that it matters much.

Happening

It may be of some small interest to elderly readers to be told of one of the accidental fruits of my researches. I find that a *happening*, which in the 1950s referred to some event like the planned break-up of some impossibly vulgar art exhibition or somebody undressing at somebody's else's *boring* party, had already been a phenomenon and a descriptive term of the Edwardian era.

Haver

Once a respectable Scottish verb meaning 'to talk nonsense', and there can never be too many words for that. Its closeness to 'hover' once gave it a useful hint of indecision, but recently, here and there, the hint has swallowed the original sense, and *haver* can now mean 'be uncertain'. Roget, however, a fair guide to usage, lists *haver* in something like its original meaning, between *waffle* and *blether*, so perhaps I need not have substituted *drivelling* for *havering* when revising a poem in 1979, and should have kept the older and better reading. *Haver* and its derivatives are best avoided by careful writers.

Having said that

This little phrase would perhaps cause less offence if less often improperly used, as in, for instance, 'Having said that, I turn now to less attractive features of his character.' The trouble comes when the words are left dangling, as in, for instance, 'Having said that, what action should be taken against him?' *Having said that* has become not much more than a classy substitute for *even so* or *nevertheless* or just *anyway*, but one with the added advantage, as some will see it, of being a fashionable phrase that manages to award the speaker marks for fairness of mind, unearned marks in most cases. Be on the safe as well as the virtuous side and never say *having said that*.

Headline English

It is no secret that newspaper headlines no longer content themselves with announcing pieces of news in abbreviated but relatively unphilistine language. Nowadays headlines come in several styles. One is the over-informative, such that not only the piece of news is given but also what followed from it, so that we learn before we start to read the story that not only has the Chancellor raised interest rates, say, but also that his doing so has 'fuelled' a Tory 'panic' about this or that. I like a headline to state straight-forward non-clever things like PRIME MINISTER ASSASSIN-ATED. To add details or consequences ahead of time is to weaken both the story and one's desire to read it, as if anyone cared.

But such matters are not my present concern; other styles of headline are. A particularly barbarous one is to take advantage of the hospitality of the language to the use of nouns as adjectives; thus an escaping couple cease to be an

ESCAPING COUPLE and become an ESCAPE COUPLE. A string of unleavened nouns will form a whole headline. Three nouns stuck cheek by jowl was once the limit, but now four is standard. Some months ago two tabloids gave their front pages to SCHOOL COACH CRASH DRAMA and SCHOOL OUTING COACH HORROR and a week or two later one of them achieved five with SCHOOL BUS BELTS SAFETY VICTORY. There is some loss of decent seriousness here, as if anyone cared.

This loss is clearer with the style of headline that uses puns or otherwise plays with words. Last month an outstandingly giggly tabloid carried the following in a single issue:

Page 1. Picture of a pretty girl who had just had a success. Caption: 'A star is born: British actress Julia Ormond gets a big part.' Headline reads, 'Movie queen is crowned', i.e. is to play Queen Guinevere in £40m King Arthur film.

2. Headline reads, 'Still on track for more rail misery'.

3. Headline reads, 'Arnie [i.e. Arnold Schwarzenegger] his true self after pregnant pause'. [His part in a recently made film had required him to simulate pregnancy.] Also headline reading, 'Career of Julia the obscure is into top Gere', i.e. the actor Richard Gere is to star as Sir Lancelot in the film. An accompanying photograph is captioned, 'Knight moves: Richard Gere makes his point [flourishes sword] while rehearsing his Lancelot swordplay.' Copy contains the sentence, 'In showbusiness terms, unknown actress Julia Ormond has found the Holy Grail.' On the same page, a large photograph of another actress is captioned, 'Dressed to thrill: . . . at premiere of new Arnie film.'

5. Headline reads, 'We're on the road to photo licences' [i.e. to the introduction of driving licences that carry a photograph of the licensee].

6–7. Headline reads, 'Crying all the way to the bank' [Barclays' profits, customers' grievances].

7. Headline reads, 'Food firms find health guide hard to stomach'.

10–11. Headline reads, 'Food firms boil over with anger as Brussels goes sour on soya milk'.

12. Headline reads, 'Banned be thy name' [a church authority has banned the use of pet-names etc. in gravestone inscriptions].

17. Headline reads, 'How our garden paradise was lost' [through nasty neighbours].

18. Headline reads, 'Border skirmish over a hedge'.

21. Heading: 'Crusoe, your island awaits'. Headline reads, 'Talking heads' [on solicitors' wigs].

23. Headline reads. 'A hot issue' [on crematoria]. Headline reads, 'Cine season'.

24. Headline reads, 'Extra time to save Graces' [statuary].

There follows a financial feature with eighteen headlines and no wordplay in ten pages.

The effect of all this in one issue is to make human concerns seem trivial to the reader. But what sort of reader is being looked for? If any, an unusual sort, one well acquainted with the Athurian legends who knows about Jude the Obscure and much else in literature and yet is at home with 'Arnie' and talking heads. And when we read of somebody headlined in this tabloid and another as 'death husband' and 'kidnap horror man', and puzzle out that the same person is meant, we may start to suspect that, as in the case of much modern poetry, the journalists concerned are not really interested in an identifiable reader. They are just playing a silly game among themselves. After all, they have to fill the paper somehow whether they have anything to say or not.

Stop Press (to use an outdated expression): The other day I read in the columns of a 'quality' newspaper – in the body of a story, not in a headline – that bird-protection societies had been set all of a twitter by something or other. Oh God, where will·it end?

Homogeneous

An ordinary, regularly formed adjective of classical parentage, meaning 'of the same kind' or 'uniform'. Begetter of the doubtful verb *homogenise*, as of milk whose cream content has been irreversibly incorporated in it, a word which would not deserve a mention but for its having produced a thriving back-formation, *homogenous* (so spelt). This, very likely pronounced with stress on the second syllable of four, is incorrect.

However

Custom has decreed that *however* should not come first in a sentence. When it does come it tends to throw an emphasis on the immediately preceding word or phrase which is very likely not wanted and may be a nuisance. If it is put first nothing much seems to go wrong, and surely one would rather write or read:

Tomorrow I go on holiday for a couple of weeks. *However*, I will telephone you as soon as I can after I get back,

than either:

Tomorrow . . . weeks. I will, *however*, telephone you . . .

or:

Tomorrow . . . weeks. I will telephone you as soon as I can after I get back, *however*.

To some tastes, however, advantageously placed (as here) or not, *however* will inevitably seem a little pompous. Why not go all the way in that direction and begin with a plonking *nevertheless*, or some way in the other and write *anyway* or *still*?

Howlers

The description covers a good deal, but I have in mind the apparently contented acceptance of an old textual blunder that has survived innumerable attempts to correct it.

So: whatever Bernard Levin thinks, *cui bono?* is not a rhetorical question meaning *Who gets anything out of this?* i.e. nobody, therefore *This is pointless*. It is a real question meaning *Who benefits from this?* i.e. *If you want to know who is behind this, consider who stands to gain.*

It is a mistake to suppose that when Hamlet says the local tradition of ceremonial drinking is a custom 'more honoured in the breach than th' observance' he means the custom is *more often* ignored than followed. He means it is *better*, more honourably, ignored than followed, as generations of verbal fops should have known. And as Shakespeare could have afforded to make a little clearer.

The sense in which an exception *proves* the rule is not the more usual one in which, for instance, Pythagoras *proved* his theorem. What an (apparent) exception does is *test* the rule. (For those who like arguments from derivation, *prove* is derived from the Latin *probare* to test, whence also *probe* and, with a changed meaning, *probable*.) Rockets are tested on *proving* grounds; a will is *proved*, achieves *probate*, when it is officially tested and found to be valid; the *proof* of an article is a test run which can be corrected; the *proof* of the pudding is in the eating. If we imagine a rule that all red-haired men are quick-tempered and an individual red-haired man is found who is not quick-tempered, the excep-

tion proves the rule when it turns out that he had in fact
dyed his naturally brown hair red.

A devil's advocate is not one who rouses to evil courses
nor one who pleads for a diabolical human being or institution. On the contrary, the *advocatus diaboli* is an elevated
ecclesiastic whose task it is to display all the sins committed
by somebody now being considered for admission to saint-
hood, thus advancing the devil's claim to be the rightful
owner of that person.

A leading question is not an important or significant one
whose answer might give away something damaging or
unusually interesting. All it does is tend to lead a court
witness to some desired reply, as a barrister might ask, 'And
the man you saw bending over the body of his victim –
was it not John Smith?' when the man in the dock is the
said J. Smith.

'Feed a cold and starve a fever.' As Robert Graves has
pointed out, this archaic source of error treats the two apparent imperatives as separate injunctions, whereas what we
have in fact is a conditional sentence: *if* you feed somebody
with a cold, he will develop a fever and then you will have
to starve him. Less prevalent since the spread of the 'show
me an X and I'll show you a Y' construction, a splendid
Americanism exemplified in 'Show me a good loser and I'll
show you a loser,' which is not a programme for two. It
came along too late to save Edith Sitwell from seeing two
apparent imperatives as separate injunctions when Lear is
made to say:

> Allow not nature more than nature needs,
> Man's life is cheap as beast's,

and reading the passage as a statement of elderly pessimism
or a couple of them.

Ilk is not a handy synonym for *gang* or *lot* or *sort* or *set*,
as in, for instance, 'Senator Joe McCarthy and his ilk'. *Ilk* is

actually a Scottish word meaning 'same', as in, for instance, 'Carrickfergus of that ilk', meaning 'Carrickfergus of Carrickfergus', i.e. of that same place. But *ilk* is to be treated with circumspection or, better, avoided altogether not because of any problem about its meaning but because it is an outmoded piece of either pedantry or ignorance. The same might be said of other expressions mentioned in this article.

Hyper-urbanisms, or between you and I

I have never saw anything like what you describe.
Elmer is no doubt your full brother but he doesn't look at all as you.
Speculation is still rife as to whom will lead the England squad in South Africa.
A rich friend has kindly asked my husband and I to dine with him wherever we please.

These examples all embody the same mistake, an indulged desire to be more correct than correct or posher than posh. A hyper-urbanism arises when a speaker puts into practice a badly taught or badly learnt lesson about the avoidance of vulgar or rustic error. Thus in the first example somebody has taken the ban on saying 'I seen' as the easier proposition that the word *seen* is to be avoided in every situation. Similarly, the word *like* is always turning up in disreputable circumstances, for example only bad people say 'It tastes good like a cigarette should' – better be on the safe side and steer clear of the word altogether. And *as* is rather posh too in its own right. Again, in the third example there can be seen a vague memory of a warning against saying 'to who', plus quite a strong feeling that *whom* is in itself an educated word. See WHOM.

But it is in the fourth example that the vice of hyper-urbanism can be seen at its starkest and also commonest. Both anecdotal impression and published figures tells us that expressions like 'between you and I and the gatepost', a venerable howler, are actually more usual today in speech and writing than the grammatical version. The origin here is probably the quite false and truly vulgar notion that to say (or write) 'It's me' is ungrammatical and therefore to be avoided. Ungrammatical it is, but completely idiomatic, and even in fun 'It is I' is too awful to be tolerated. Anyway, the impression lingers in some that 'me' is rather mean and low and uneducated, whereas 'I' is dignified, upmarket and sort of Oxford-accented *in itself*. This view of style might have had the word 'stilted' – i.e. on stilts, artificially elevated – coined specially for it.

It remains true that the best writers are not always the best models. In a famous speech in *Julius Caesar* Cassius tells Brutus:

I had as lief not be as live to be
In awe of such a thing as I myself [i.e. a man, i.e. Caesar]

which shows the old boy between-you-and-I-ing like an American college graduate, unless perhaps the suggestion is that Cassius has something stilted in his character, which I have always rather felt. Later in the same speech, Cassius follows my example 2 in talking of the time Caesar was ill with a fever and called to a friend for a thirst-quencher 'as a sick girl'.

Hyphen

This word comes from two Greek words together meaning 'under one', which gets nobody anywhere and merely prompts the reflection that argument by etymology only serves the purpose of intimidating ignorant antagonists. On, then.

This is one more case in which matters have not improved since Fowler's day, since he wrote in 1926:

> The chaos prevailing among writers or printers or both regarding the use of hyphens is discreditable to English education . . . The wrong use or wrong non-use of hyphens makes the words, if strictly interpreted, mean something different from what the writers intended. It is no adequate answer to such criticisms to say that actual misunderstanding is unlikely; to have to depend on one's employer's readiness to take the will for the deed is surely a humiliation that no decent craftsman should be willing to put up with.

And so say all of us who may be reading this book. The references there to 'printers' needs updating to something like 'editors', meaning those who declare copy fit to print. Such people now often get it wrong by preserving in mid-column a hyphen originally put at the end of a line to signal a word-break: *inter-fere*, say, is acceptable split between lines but not as part of a single line. This mistake is comparatively rare and seldom causes confusion; even so, time spent wondering whether an *exactor* may not be an *ex-actor* is time avoidably wasted.

The hyphen is properly and necessarily used to join the halves of a two-word adjectival phrase, as in *fair-haired children*, *last-ditch resistance*, *falling-down drunk*, *over-familiar reference*. Breaches of this rule are rare and not troublesome.

Hyphens are also required when a phrase of more than two words is used adjectivally, as in *middle-of-the-road policy*, *too-good-to-be-true story*, *no-holds-barred contest*.

No hard-and-fast rule can be devised that lays down when a two-word phrase is to be hyphenated and when the two words are to be run into one, though there will be a rough consensus that, for example, *book-plate* and *bookseller* are each properly set out and that *bookplate* and *book-seller* might seem respectively new-fangled and fussy.

A hyphen is not required when a normal adverb (i.e. one ending in *-ly*) plus an adjective or other modifier are used in an adjectival role, as in *Jack's equally detestable brother, a beautifully kept garden, her abnormally sensitive hearing*. A hyphen is required, however, when the adverb lacks a final *-ly*, like *well, ill, seldom, altogether* or one of those words like *tight* and *slow* that double as adjectives. To avoid ambiguity here we must write *a well-kept garden, an ill-considered objection, a tight-fisted policy*.

The commonest fault in the use of the hyphen, and the hardest to eradicate, is found when an adjectival phrase is used predicatively. So a gent may write of *a hard-to-conquer* mountain peak but not of a mountain peak that remains *hard-to-conquer, an often-proposed* solution but not of one that is *often-proposed*. For some reason this fault is especially common when numbers, including fractions, are concerned, and we read every other day of criminals being imprisoned for *two-and-a-half years*, a woman becoming a *mother-of-three* and even of some unfortunate being stabbed *six-times*. And the Tories have been in power for a *decade-and-a-half*.

Finally, there seems no end to the list of common phrases that some berk will bung a superfluous hyphen into the middle of: *artificial-leg, daily-help, false-teeth, taxi-firm, martial-law, rainy-day, airport-lounge, first-wicket, piano-concerto, lung-cancer, cavalry-regiment, overseas-service*. I hope I need not add that of course one none the less writes of *a false-teeth problem*, a *first-wicket stand*, etc.

The only guide is: omit the hyphen whenever possible, so avoid not only *mechanically propelled vehicle users* (a beauty from *MEU*) but also *a man eating tiger*. And *no one* is right and *no-one* is wrong.

I

Idiom

Idiom, or devotion to idiom, or robust preference for idiom over what reason and common sense may clearly indicate, is what keeps English people or speakers of English saying and writing *I won't be any longer than I can help* when what the fellow so obviously and notoriously means is *I won't be any longer than I can't help*. Idiom, defined in the *COD* as a 'form of expression peculiar to a language' and translated by Fowler from the original Greek word as 'a manifestation of the peculiar', is a good blanket defence of the otherwise indefensible in phraseology, but should not be pushed too far. Idiom, or appeals to the dictates of idiom, may allow us to keep on writing and saying *I shouldn't be surprised if it didn't come on to rain* without anybody turning a hair, but it was naughty of Milton to write,

> Adam, the goodliest man of men since born
> His sons, the fairest of her daughters Eve.

These famous lines, which nobody else could or would have written, produce two successive forms of discomfort in the reader, who first wonders uneasily whether some little-known but real English idiom justifies their double affront to common sense, and then wonders almost as uneasily whether some rather better-known Latin construction is being invoked. If Milton did not surmise as much he should have done, and never mind that guff about fit audience, though few.

Idiom, or the citing of idiom, remains a good protection against the charge of pedantry, but its hold on the mind shows signs of weakening. In the same week I heard a broadcaster say that Snooks had had a *heyday* (hay-day?) on the cricket field, when Snooks may or may not have been in his heyday but had actually had a *field*-day; and then I was told over the air that a senior musician had visited the opera on sudden impulse 'only to find' that his star ex-pupil was conducting the orchestra – but no, the English idiom demands that that form of words should be followed only by a *disagreeable* surprise, like the performance having been cancelled or the building burnt down.

Such lapses in idiom are by definition invulnerable to logic and are no doubt often imputable to a foreigner's knowledge of English, perfect in every respect, perhaps, but for that of idiomatic grasp. Such minor inexactitudes are to be expected when a national language becomes international too.

No such excuse is available for the failures to get it right increasingly heard over the air and in speech. Native speakers are now uncertain of English idiom, for instance not knowing the difference between *on my own behalf*, *on my own account* and *for my own part*. Such differences may be hard to tie down but they were once instantly recognisable. They become blurred when nobody really cares much what is being said.

If and when

'Any writer who uses this formula,' says Fowler, 'lays himself open to entirely reasonable suspicions on the part of his reader.' That reader must lead an anxious life. No doubt use of the formula can be evidence of a lazy disinclination on the writer's part to decide which case of the two is being considered, but the harm done thereby, if any, is small, too small perhaps to justify the writing (or reading) of a couple of earnest columns on the point. And surely such a writer may have been moved less by laziness than by a desire not to commit his reader to an exclusive if or when.

Other authorities have castigated the 'and/or' formula, requiring the writer to make up his mind between 'and' and 'or'. Well, the whole thing may look ugly on the page, especially the medial oblique stroke or oblique or stroke or virgule or, by a brisk Americanism, slash. But as a neat and clear way of expressing 'either *and* or *or* depending which fits' it has no equals, and as with 'if and when' it saves the writer from having to be definite. I myself have not long ago taken to writing 'and-or', perhaps unwisely.

Fowler is also a bit harsh with 'unless and until'.

Imply, infer

Nothing could prevent this soporific duo from coming to the surface sooner or later in any discussion of this sort. It was established years ago that history was no help, that *imply* once meant, among other things, to attribute, as when you *implied* a motive to someone or a meaning to some statement, and *infer* often meant then what *imply* means now, to suggest strongly, to mean without actually saying. And so on.

It seems best to cut through all this by stating categorically that nowadays *imply* describes a transmitting process and *infer* describes a receiving process: I *imply*, you *infer*. Smoke *implies* fire; you *infer* the presence of fire from seeing and/or smelling smoke, an eminently clear and comprehensible arrangement.

There is only one difficulty. *Imply* is straightforward enough; nobody ever gets that wrong. But now and then some clot will ask you in conversation if you mean to *infer* that he is drunk when you have probably not even *implied* that he is. He gets that one wrong not for any interesting historical reason but merely because he is a great one for getting things wrong. How you deal with him is your own affair, but just try to remember that *imply* comes from a Latin word meaning to fold in and *infer* from another one meaning to go into or induce. I mention these ancient roots not because I think etymologies generally give true meanings but because in this case they may assist memory. If you feel you have mental room for only one of the two, stick to *infer* while you wait for a new head.

Important

Section 137 in my Roget's *Thesaurus* is headed Occasion: timelessness. Within it there are a couple of lines in the Adjective subsection reading:

> *crucial*, critical, key, momentous, climactic, pivotal, decisive 638 *important*,

and on duly turning to section 638 (Importance) we find, in the Adjective subsection there, a block of fifty-seven adjectives beginning with *important* and including several that might have been found in 137's list but are not.

The notions of urgency and of importance, though often found together, are distinguishable. To pick up a taxi may be urgent, especially in the rain, but it is probably unimportant. The survival of the human race is important, perhaps, but it seems at the moment not to be an urgent problem. An issue genuinely uniting the two is rather rare, much rarer than a reader of letters to the Press, for instance, is led to believe. Every issue is said to be a key issue, every possible decision is crucial, critical, pivotal, essential, vital.

At the moment, *key* is perhaps the brand leader; it appeals so strongly to an MP that he uses the adjective twice over in the same sentence (in a letter to *The Times* today).

My memory takes me back fifty years to northern France, where the volume of signal traffic became so huge that urgency markings seemed to have lost their meaning, and bundles of emergency-operations messages were sent off on the ordinary dispatch-rider run. The reader will recall that we won the war notwithstanding all the fuss about urgency. The content of the message is what counts, not the priority stamped on it. One day, when key issues and crucial decisions are no more, it might be possible to say that something is *important*, incidentally the lowest priority marking of them all.

In- and un-

It looks a bit berkish to get these prefixes muddled and write, for instance, *undiscriminate* and *indiscriminating*, but unfortunately there is no rule. It might be thought that anyone used to reading, writing and hearing English would know as if instinctively when to use *in-* and when *un-*, and indeed this is usually so. Not always, however, and experience will suggest that some people's instinct is more fallible than others'.

The only safe treatment of what may seem a small problem is to consult the dictionary if ever you feel less than absolutely certain, and some writers had better grit their teeth and check everything less obviously cast-iron than *unlikely* or *incessant*. In the absence of a dictionary or a safe alternative word or any other way round the difficulty, pick *un-* at the start of what looks like an English-based word like *unspeakable*. If you are going to be wrong, be wrong in your own language.

In a few minutes

Servants and other inferior persons have from time imme-
morial been promising they will follow an order by saying,
or shouting from near by, something that means 'at once'
and then dawdling or delaying indefinitely. Following their
progress, or the lack of it, expressions that formerly meant
'at once' have come to mean 'in a little while'. The most
famous of these is *presently*.

Before getting to grips with the adverb, we might take
a moment over the adjective *present*, which the biblical 'God
is . . . a very *present* help in trouble' uses to mean not only
that he is always present or available but also that he comes
to our aid at once. *Presently* itself on its early appearances
in the fifteenth century meant 'immediately, instantly', but
before the end of the sixteenth had settled down to the
meaning it still retains, 'before long'. Less notorious examples of the same process include *anon* (*see you anon* today
means 'see you some time or other, if then'), *by and by* and
even *soon*, though you have to go back as far as to the Old
English ancestor of the last word to be sure of finding the
unequivocal sense 'at once'. *Now*, as in 'I'll fetch your drinks
now,' was going the same way as *presently* in South Wales
when last heard of. And finally, having dallied with *after
the break, in a couple of minutes* and such palliatives, TV
declares boldly *next on LCM television* when they mean not
by any means next but after a stiff dose of trailers and
advertisements.

Human beings need their little lazinesses and dis-
honesties, and a world in which everything was understood
to mean what it said, no more nor less, would be intolerable.
For all that, a world in which nothing ever happened
straight away, in which that very concept had been lost,
would not be much fun either.

In excess of

This dreadful little cluster has somehow insinuated itself into serious contexts in which precise quantities are bandied about. Where it was once considered careful enough to write of temperatures in the 80s or over 80° it now seems requisite to talk about temperatures *in excess of* 80 degrees. If *over* is somehow ruled out, *more than* will do, anything to avoid this fussy piece of pseudo-accuracy which contributes nothing but length and a fraudulent scientistic glow. I think I once heard talk about a dose of some opiate of *up to in excess of* so many grains, but am probably imagining things.

Infamous, infamy

Both adjective and noun used to be terms of extreme moral disapproval, equivalent in depth of feeling to 'abominable' and 'wickedness'. Then quite recently, perhaps not before the 1980s, the adjective weakened in severity to something on the level of 'notorious'. A biography of that period describes its subject's undergraduate life at Oxford in the 1920s as 'now infamous'. In former days, till recently as I say, you or your behaviour were registered as infamous at the time and you or it stayed that way; the notion of becoming infamous long afterwards was meaningless. Round about ten years ago, the account of an interview with a supposedly unconventional lady writer called her 'infamous' in its headline, and I remember thinking she had quite enough money already without the vast sum she would surely win at her libel action. But nothing happened because there was no court action; possibly no sufficiently reactionary legal figure was available.

The noun *infamy*, although seemingly out of use, retains its former meaning, but *infamous* is now unusable through ambiguity.

Internecine

Pronounced intuhNEEsine. According to *COD*, the word now means 'mutually destructive' and, according to observation, 'internally destructive' into the bargain, as in 'internecine conflict'. Perhaps meanly, I hope to give complacent would-be purists a momentary twinge by telling them that the *inter* prefix here, as in *interficio*, 'I kill', stands for *thoroughly*, not *reciprocally*, and that the nearest Latinate adjectives to what they want are *intestine* and good old *internal*. Or *civil*, as in *civil war*.

Into

Well, *into* is a word although *onto* is not, or not yet. Nevertheless we now and then *read* into where *in to* is probably meant or should have been written, as in, say, *Then we went into where the others were.* Those who produce a printed version of what we have written are inclined to follow the would-be vivid fashion of printing as one word what was intended to be two, hence many a *worthwhile* and *forever* that started life as *worth while* and *for ever*. I merely draw attention to another thing to look out for in proof-correcting.

The use of *into* as shorthand for 'actively interested in', as in, say, *He's into Georgian silver plate*, seems handy and harmless to me, though it is admittedly trendy, or was.

Ironical

It used to be said with some meaning that things like abrupt, spectacular but somehow appropriate reversals of fortune were ironical, partaking of irony in a sense well defined in *COD* as:

ill-timed or perverse arrival of event or circumstance in
itself desirable, due to the feigned good will and actual
malice of (Fate, circumstance etc.),

though it might be fair to add that the arrival of misfortune
hard upon some exceptional success would also have been
accounted irony, or an irony. Thus the diagnosis of terminal
cancer in a young man crippled from birth, now newly
embarked on a promising career in law, was probably called
ironical among other things by some of those concerned.

Recently all seriousness seems to have departed from the
word. The slightest and most banal coincidence or point
of resemblance or even just-perceptible absence of one,
unworthy of a single grunt of interest, gets called ironical.
The other day I read somewhere of how ironical it was that
the going at last year's particular horse-race was perceptibly
either better or worse than that predicted this year, I forget
which.

-ise and -ize

In the past, a great deal of ink was spilt on the derivations,
differentiations, etc., of these two verb-terminations. Fowler
characteristically recommends using -*ise* at all times while
on another page supplying a list of twenty-one of the 'more
important' verbs that must never take the Z even if -*ize* 'is
accepted as the normal form'. Nowadays you may use -*ise*
yourself everywhere without a second thought. But keep
your eye out for horrible coinages like *tenderise* – of meat
or something resembling meat – and *deratise* – to rid (a
building etc.) of rats. The latter is as genuine a specimen
as the former; indeed I once saw *deratisation* in print.

J

Jargon

This word, of unknown origin, has several near-synonyms and any attempt to distinguish them is perilous. *Jargon* itself has at least two separable meanings, as follows:

1. With another word or two limiting it to a group, a trade, etc., as in *sociologists' jargon*, *art-critics' jargon*, etc., using a specialised vocabulary.
2. Without such limitation, as in *then he lapsed into jargon*, *you're talking pure jargon*, etc., partly unintelligible and unpleasant to listen to. Perhaps (1) as heard by an outsider, one not in the group.

Argot is best kept for French slang if the word is to be used in English at all.

Cant has at least two separable meanings, as follows:

1. Hypocritical moralistic attitudinising (*his speech was full of cant about duty*, etc.)
2. Much as *jargon* 1, language, vocabulary limited to a group (*thieves' cant*, etc.).

Dialect I have treated separately.

Lingo is a contemptuous or jocose term for a foreign language. Once used by insecure Oxonian philologists to refer to Old English, Middle English, etc.

Patois now has at least two separable meanings, as follows:

1. Rustic or corrupt urban speech, best kept for forms of French (whence pronunciation PATwah), especially in old New Orleans and the area round about.
2. A trendy near-synonym of *jargon* 1 and *cant* 2.

Pidgin is a large subject, especially since what were once called forms of pidgin English have passed through stages of creolisation and become the official languages of new nations in the Pacific and elsewhere. The term *pidgin*, said to have originated in an Oriental attempt to pronounce the English word *business*, and not so long ago an imprecise term fit for unserious use, is now highly specialised and to be applied with caution. Nevertheless it can be predicted that, if an official language other than English emerges in South Africa, it will have pidgin features, as Afrikaans has always had.

Slang, a word of unknown origin. Where discoverable, the origins of this amorphous conglomeration of words and expressions must lie in some kinds of private language in school or regiment or comparable group. Not much more can sensibly be said, except perhaps that on one side slang connects with *jargon* 1 and *cant* 2 to mean something semi-private, and on the other abuts on mere informality. What is a slang phrase and what is no more than informal, and therefore freely available to all, is sometimes a distinction difficult to draw. There never was a more useful dictionary example than the one given in *COD* (1988 edn.) against *brolly*: *n.* 1. (colloq.) umbrella. 2. (sl.) parachute.

Jargon 2001

Here are two advertisements that appeared in a London newspaper in the year 1994.

SENIOR VICE PRESIDENT – FASHION-LED RETAIL

This is a challenging opportunity to join a fast-growing, customer-focused business which although a major player in fashion retail, is entering an evolutionary stage in its development, with the aim of building a team that will lead the group forward into the twenty-first century.

Probably in your mid thirties and educated to degree level, you will be a dynamic leader with the strategic vision to steer the business through an exciting stage of its development. You will already have an extensive product and buying background in womenswear, together with an impressive record of high achievement in a similar role with a major multi-site fashion operation.

Your energy, enthusiasm and assured interpersonal skills will be supported by a proven ability to think laterally and manage positive change. You will also display the potential for further career advancement.

DEVELOPMENT MANAGER – STRATEGIC ACCOUNTS

The company
– UK division of world class multinational. Exceptional growth, highly profitable.
– Manufacturer of global brand supported by highly original advertising/marketing.
– Strong culture that actively encourages open dialogue, staff empowerment and team results.

The position
– Proactively work with major customers, building mutually beneficial partnerships.

- Act as strategist and facilitator, coordinating internal and external resources to achieve business objectives.
- Continuously manage the review and analysis of retail data and forecasts to optimise product placement.

Qualifications
- Bright, numerate graduate, with retail or related experience in account management/buying/merchandising.
- Clear understanding of supply chain management.
- Proven managerial skills, ability to delegate effectively. Mature, balanced approach with exceptional interpersonal skills.

Jejune

If I say this maltreated word has ceased to be current, I can more or less confidently predict, language-users being what they are, its reappearance tomorrow. But I have not come across any fresh uses of *jejune*, good, bad or indifferent, since my intended demolition-job of 1980. I wrote then that 'here was my favourite solecism of all time' (still true) and continue to find it highly educative. Accordingly I now summarise and paraphrase my earlier reconstruction of the word's progress to enormity:

STAGE I: A writes: 'His arguments are unoriginal and jejune.' (A knows that 'jejune' means 'thin, unsatisfying', a rare word, admittedly, but one with a nice ring to it.)
STAGE II: B notices the nice ring. He doesn't know what the word means and of course wouldn't dream of consulting a dictionary even if he possessed one. There is something vaguely French as well as nice about the ring to 'jejune'; in fact now he comes to think of it it reminds him of 'jeune', which he knows means 'young'. Peering at the context, he sees that 'jejune' could mean, if not exactly

'young', then something like 'un-grown-up, immature, callow'. Hooray! – he's always needing words for that, and here's a new one, one of superior quality, too.

STAGE III: B starts writing stuff like 'Much of the dialogue is *jejune*, in fact downright childish.' With the latest edition of *COD* giving 'puerile' as a sense of 'jejune', the story might be thought to be over, but there is one further stage.

STAGE IV: Having 'jeune' in their heads, people who have never seen the word in print start pronouncing 'jejune' not 'djiJOON' but 'zherZHERN', in the apparent belief that French people always give a tiny stutter when they say 'jeune'. (I have heard 'zherZHERN' several times in the last few years.) Finally C takes the inevitable step of writing *jejeune* (I have seen several examples), or even, just that much better: 'Although the actual arguments are a little *jéjeune*, the staging of the mass scenes are [*sic*] impressive.' Italics in original! – which with the acute accent in place set the seal on the deportation of an English word into French, surely a unique event.

I ended my exposition with a kind of footnote:

> For the interested, 'jejune' is indeed connected with a French word, but it is 'jeune' with distinguishing circumflex over the U until such diacritical remarks were abolished a few years ago. Both this 'jeune' and 'jejune' derive from the Latin '[dies] ieiuna' or 'jejuna', a 'fast [day]'. Hence the familiar 'déjeuner', to de-fast as we break-fast. 'Jejune' then first meant 'fast-like, scanty, Lenten', like the entertainment Rosencrantz feared the players would receive from Hamlet.

Judgemental

This is a vogue-word from the more popular fringes of psychology. A *judgemental* person or attitude is one inclined to pass judgements on other people and their actions, in practice often unfavourable judgements and therefore much to be reprehended. Possibly the reprehension is emphasised by the location of the main stress on the second syllable of the word, thus subtly suggesting that the afflicted person is 'mental' in the colloquial sense. I should have thought on the contrary that being (unfavourably) judgemental about things like murder and people like Stalin was required by sanity as well as decency; tolerance for the tolerable and intolerance for the intolerable.

Just desserts

There are three nouns, *desert* with stress on first syllable, meaning a desolate region, *desert* with stress on second, meaning in the plural what somebody deserves, and *dessert* with stress also on second, meaning the sweet course of a main meal. Everybody knows that so well that to set it down here may seem needless. But if it really is needless, why do people keep writing about Joe Bloggs getting his [just] desserts when no pun can possibly have been intended? Because such writers have become *pun-drunk*, as they might put it themselves on a goodish day. It does seem time to look out when they let puns or the vague memory of puns get between them and the language, or them and reason.

K

Kafka's *The Castle*

The above is the sort of thing people never say but apparently make no bones about writing when they have something to impart from Kafka and *The Castle*, a suspicious divergence. Speakers of English understandably feel that a noun, or modifier-plus-noun, will take a maximum of one article or possessive or other handle and shy away from saying anything like 'Graham Greene's *The Confidential Agent*' or 'Anthony Burgess's *A Clockwork Orange*' or 'A.N. Other's *He Fell Among Thieves*'. What doomed the efforts of *The Times* to get itself called *The Times* in all circumstances was of course the refusal of people even to write 'The newspaper is neither your *The Times* nor my *The Times* but Rupert Murdoch's *The Times*,' and still less to dream of saying things like 'Do you do the *The Times* crossword?'

To behave properly you have to write, for instance, 'Graham Greene's thriller, *The Confidential Agent*' and 'Anthony Burgess's fantasy of the future, *A Clockwork Orange*' and 'Kafka's novel [or whatever it is] *The Castle*'. Until quite recently it looked as if you could write of Greene's *Confidential Agent* and Burgess's *Clockwork Orange* and Kafka's *Castle*, but indexers unnecessarily and pissily put a stop to that by throwing *The* and *A* and so on back in front of the main body of the title. Nowadays you must either stick in a category-label like 'novel' or 'play' or write about works felt to be too old to need a precursory article, like Shakespeare's *Tempest* or Hardy's *Mayor of Casterbridge*. Or write something you would never contemplate saying. Or cunningly recast the sentence.

Kids

This word for *children*, labelled an Americanism by *COD*, was until about 1970 entirely colloquial and conversational, with no special overtones. Then it started to become a teachers' and educators' term for *schoolchildren*, featured in the boast, 'We [in our dedicated way] don't teach subjects, we teach kids.' It now turns up in serious places like the letters page in *The Times*, if that is a serious place. *Kids* in this sense will fade soon, though not soon enough to suit me.

My objection to its 'committed' use is not to be traced, I hope, to my being snooty, old-fashioned, old or British. No, this use carries a strong hint of being down-to-earth on purpose (see BELLY). It condescends to children and robs them of their dignity in just the same way as it denatures an Italian, say, to call him a wop.

To me, dubbing children *kids* out of policy recalls the affected, chummy docking of Christian names for public use at the head of articles and such and even at the foot of letters to *The Times*. Let me be the one to decide when if ever to address you or refer to you as Chris, Ken, Dave or Jim.

Kilometre

Perhaps sadly, perhaps not, this is hardly the place to launch an attack on the metric system. I can, however, legitimately snipe at the habit of stressing the word *kilometre* on the second syllable, thus turning the thing into a device for measuring thousands, as an anemometer measures wind-force and a hygrometer measures humidity. Once upon a time there was indeed a true kilometer, built on the orders of one of the ancient Persian kings. Tired of guessing how many men there were in his army and unable to trust anybody to estimate them, his majesty had a thousand such men counted out, which was feasible, and had a wall built round them. Filling and emptying this a few hundred times got the King a near-enough answer to his problem.

Not many people know that, or would care if they did.

L

Lather

As long as I can remember I have known, or been told, that *lather* rhymes with *gather* and not *father*, and like everybody else I go on doing as before and pronounce the wretched (and seldom needed) word as I always have, to rhyme with *father*. At the rate we seem to be going with shaving-cream and machine washing of clothes, dishes, etc., both thing and word will soon have fallen out of use. What happened to the first syllable of *solder*?

Letters or figures

A journalist recently lamented the seeming fact that 'among the 231 million inhabitants of the United States there were not even 3 or 4,000 who might be interested in [his] life story'. That at least was what appeared in print. What the man actually wrote had obviously pertained to three or four thousand people who might or might not have been interested, but some officious intermediary had turned it into nonsense.

Numbers expressed in words, as four thousand people or a hundred reasons, are not necessarily intended to be precise. Those expressed in figures cannot help seeming as if they are so intended. The title of Ian Hay's account of the beginning of the Great War, *The First Hundred Thousand*, meant something quite different from what *The First 100,000* would have meant. What until the other day was a firm distinction is now being eroded.

Other agents of this erosion are the practice of printing, for instance, '£4.3m' for '£4,300,000' but continuing to set, for instance, '£43,000' in full. The apparent rule whereby a number coming first in a sentence must be spelt out in words leads straight to nonsense, as in 'Nineteen-forty-five, unlike 1950, gave Labour a comfortable majority in the House.' Another apparent rule binds broadcasters, such that 'one hundred' must always be said instead of 'a hundred', producing nonsenses like 'a one-hundred-pound bottle of wine'.

Nowadays more and more people are innumerate, very likely know which is the bigger of a million and ten thousand but would not much care to have to write out the two of them in figures, and so are more vulnerable than their parents to confusion over quantities. Some may even feel dimly that knowing about such things is better left to computers. Conspiracies are unlikely things but unorganised consensuses are less so, and if there exists one to degrade the importance of quantities it comes at an infectious time.

Like

All of us know that *like* is to be avoided in conjunctional uses, or at least not to say 'he behaved like he was drunk' etc., and nearly all of us have heard about the hippie who called 'Like help' when he was near drowning. No wonder some of us avoid the word even when the circumstances call for it (see HYPER-URBANISMS). No linguistic ban is better known. Unfortunately the picture, like many a linguistic picture, is a little complicated.

Only a little: of the important two complicators, one is that people use the like-in-conjunctional use frequently in conversation, even if they tend to avoid it in writing; and the other is that some of them feel uneasily that there may be something unnatural, even pedantic, in its too-obvious avoidance. A third factor, that there is an impressive list of accepted writers who have used this *like* in the past, probably cuts little ice in itself, though it may be dimly felt that it must be better to be wrong with Shakespeare than right with Professor Tomnoddy. Two quite strong desires, not to seem mincingly donnish and not to be or look illiterate and philistine, pull in opposite directions.

My solution is in two parts, conversational and written:

1. Forget that you are not supposed to talk about something or other tasting good like a cigarette should. The possible disapproval of a self-appointed arbiter of spoken usage is not much to be feared.
2. Continue to avoid conjunctional *like* on paper; you may not know quite what a conjunction is but you know how it feels. But always remember Orwell's final decree: break any stylistic rule rather than commit a barbarity – which includes all forms of conscious unnaturalness, not least those resulting from hankering after correctitude.

Long or short?

Few people are perfectly consistent in their speech. I for one am never sure how to pronounce the I in words like *direct*: should it be long, like *eye*, or short, as in *pin*? Or rather I was not sure till I looked it up in *COD*, where I found what I had more or less foreseen, that either value, long or short, was accepted and recommended, both for *direct* itself and for all its derivatives, like *directorate*. I frankly had not foreseen the equal endorsement of both values in the third syllable of *civilisation*, for instance, at least in a

British dictionary. American usage, as testified by observation and by American dictionaries, leans definitely but not exclusively towards a short vowel in such words.

It seems that this is not a matter that invites the laying down of the law. For all that, I suggest the following. If you want to be emphatic and have no fear of perhaps being thought a little bit ossified and careful and British, use the long vowel. In all other circumstances use the short. For once we have here a matter of taste.

M

Major

Apart from special cases like Ursa Major, major-general, the key of C major and a few phrases relating to surgery, operations, etc., this word needs treating with caution. It is an indefinite comparative, coming straight from Latin where it is the comparative of *magnus*, 'great'. It seems hard to justify *major* at all in its popular sense of *outstanding, unusually important*. As applied to practitioners of the fine arts the word is tendentious. When the phrase *major poet* or *major composer* is used of some individual, the user is making an assertion that is not an assertion, a claim that need not be defended or argued for because nothing of substance has been claimed. 'Snooks takes his place among the major artists of our time' is saying as much and as little as 'Blanco washes whiter'.

To apply the adjective *great* to an artist may be perilous but is not empty, there being criteria to be argued over. As for *important*, this seems to me to lurch towards blurb-writer's commendation in the *major* style – as important as who, more important than who else? I myself would want to add that artistic importance is not very important, far less so than the question of whether a sonnet or a sonata is any *good*. To deserve that description is hard enough.

Major as in *major portion of* (= greater or larger or large part of), like *the majority of* (= most of), is nothing worse than empty pomposity.

The Mall, Pall Mall

The thoroughfare in St James's Park has a name pronounced to rhyme with *gal* or *shall* and there is no argument about that. The street between Trafalgar Square and St James's Palace has a name now pronounced like *pal* followed by *mall* as above and there is still argument or at least disagreement about that. Undoubtedly the pronunciation was once like *pell-mell*, though the two expressions are apparently not related, and some older speakers still preserve the original pronunciation, as the *COD* did until 1970. It is safe to say that by the early years of the next century no one will be saying the name like *pell-mell* (rhyming with *gel* for *girl*).

Explanations for linguistic change, even minor ones like this, are likely to be fanciful or non-existent, but in the present case I would venture something to do with social change. As the *COD* says, Pall Mall was 'noted for clubs', meaning originally gentlemen's clubs whose membership was upper class. As that membership expanded downwards socially to include people like me (born 1922), so perhaps did pronunciations like that of *Pall Mall*. Gentlemen, unlike those less fortunately placed, notoriously take no heed of what you think of them, not least whether a favoured pronunciation of theirs might strike some hearers as affected or exclusive. As the middle classes moved into the clubs of Pall Mall and became predominant in them, so perhaps the accepted pronunciation of the name of the place correspondingly changed. Fanciful, as I said, but possible all the same.

Malnutrition

Fowler's entry under this head is a prime example of what, in a less august personage, might be called his insensitivity or even his philistinism, not to mention his ignorance. Malnutrition is *not* the same as underfeeding, but means the state of being badly or unwisely or for any reason inadequately supplied with sustaining food, not underfed. The British working classes before and indeed after the late war often had plenty to eat, but it was mostly food like white bread, crisps, biscuits, tinned fruit and jam, filling perhaps but not part of a healthy diet.

May and might

This entry would not have been needed until quite recently, but writers in the public prints seem never to tire in their quest for new illiteracies. This one is easily detected and avoided. Not many people used to reading could fail to spot that something is wrong in the sentence *If Napoleon had been at his best on the day of Waterloo, the result of the battle may have been different*, and almost as few would not feel, however dimly, that the writer has managed to imply that the actual result is unknown, perhaps unknowable. Substitute *might* for *may* and history and sanity are restored. Most writers would never dream of erring in this shoddy way. The remainder, the weaker brethren, will just have to put *may–might* on their list of danger-spots.

While we are on *might*, journalists have taken to saying things like, *This climbdown could signal a further Tory defeat*, perhaps out of a lubberly sense of caution. I want to shriek, 'Of course it *could*! Just as it *could* signal Balls to Mr Banglestein! *Might*, you numskull, *might*!' But I seldom do.

Meaningful

Until recently this word, if it is a word at all, was used by philosophers and others to distinguish a verifiable or disprovable statement or question from one that was in this sense meaningless. Thus 'It's Thursday today' is meaningful,

'It's a beautiful day' is (in this sense) meaningless. Then some uneducated person took *meaningful* for a longer and therefore posher variant of the old adjective *meaning* as in 'She gave him a meaning look', in others words a look charged with meaning, an expressive or significant look. In a trice people were giving each other meaningful looks and suchlike all over the shop, and not thinking of any verifiable or disprovable looks either. So, by a familiar process, both *meaning* and *meaningful* became unusable by careful writers.

Medieval

Now the standard spelling. Pronounced in four syllables as 'meddy-eeval', with please no glottal stop before the second E. To pronounce in three syllables as 'medd-eeval' or 'mee-deeval' is an infallible sign of fundamental illiteracy, a positive shibboleth.

Membership

Any trade unionist (it is nearly always a trade unionist rather than, say, a club secretary) who talks about his *membership* when he means his *members* is suffering from, among other things, an inflated ego. The case is different when he means *number* of members, and a clause like 'our membership has doubled [or halved] in the last five years' is perfectly innocuous, but the other shows undisguised preference for the supposed grander word.

Merry Christmas

It may betray excessive zeal to look for solecisms on a Christmas card, but here goes. The form of words above this brief article is the correct one, so never anywhere write

Xmas for *Christmas* and also never print or write what many now do, *Happy* Christmas. *Merry* means among other things 'given over to merrymaking or becoming merry, perhaps with the assistance of alcohol', a festive interval in the yearly round. There is a connection with the word *mirth*. In the past you went on to wish somebody 'a happy and prosperous New Year'. Unlike *merry*, *happy* connotes a settled state, one that might well last a whole year. But whether Christmas be merry or happy, remember not to pronounce the T in it.

Meticulous

Fowler devotes nearly a thousand of his own words to this one word, which he calls 'wicked', strong language for him, and shows unarguably that its Latin original, *meticulosus*, meant something quite different from its present sense, *beset by small fears* as against *punctilious*. He traces its appearance in English to the French Academy dictionary of 1835, and goes on, 'The question is whether we are going to allow the word to be imposed upon us for general use, now that the journalist of the daily papers has caught it up from the literary critic,' and proceeds to put the case against our giving such permission, rounding things off with one quotation illustrating the correct use of the word and a dozen of the incorrect. There was undoubtedly a twinkle in Fowler's eye as he stated his question, though it is almost as clear that he was in earnest too, wishing at least that grammarians and lexicographers should indeed be the select body to admit new usages to language. But he must have known too that, by whatever process it may be that such usages get their start, 'we', the learned few, are never even consulted. Hence we should not be surprised to read in the fifth edition of *COD* that *meticulous* principally means 'overscrupulous about minute details'; the seventh edition hangs a pair of brackets round the over-.

The cause, as always is lost. So what can it be that prevents me from going on using the word at all?

Much, very

I once came across the sentence *Suddenly he was very afraid* in a story in a pulp magazine, to be sure, but it would be patronising, however natural, to lower one's standards to suit the company. Anyway, that *very afraid* bothered me. Something was wrong, but what? Following a rule I had learnt even longer ago, I mentally substituted *much* for *very* and found I had replaced one discomfort with another. However 'correct' *he was much afraid* might be, it seemed stiff and starchy, all wrong in a thrillerish context, and sticking *very* back in front of *much* only made matters worse. I soon saw that it was *afraid* that was wrong and that nobody could object to *he was very frightened.*

This small incident taught me something. The rule about true adjectives going with *very* (*I thought she was very attractive*) while mere participles required *much* (*The old lady was much encouraged*) evidently had its limitations. But not only that. The fact that a word or phrase satisfies one set of criteria is no guarantee that it satisfies all. And not only that, either. If a sentence keeps all the rules you know and still seems wrong, change it. That takes longer, but so does anything worth while.

N

Noisome

This is a rather fancy word meaning 'objectionable, offensive, evil-smelling', nothing to do with *noise* (the S of *noisome* is unvoiced), more to do with *annoy*. What it is really doing in this dictionary is carrying my money as the likeliest tip for the solecism of 1996 or so. Any day now the eye of some verbal mountebank will catch *noisome* and the harmless dissyllable will be transmogrified into a posh near-enough synonym for *noisy*, as happened to *fulsome*, now used like a posh word for *full* (see FULSOME). Mark my words.

Nor

Sometimes, if the sentence is long enough and the writer negligent enough, *or* gets used round about half way where grammar and common sense would demand *nor*. The point of calling for vigilance here is not just the preservation of grammatical usage, though there is that, but also saving the time and trouble of the type of reader who has to trudge back to make certain that *nor* was actually required. So, outside a short-term, tea-or-coffee choice, be careful with *or*.

Not un-

In his article *Politics and the English Language* (1946), a vigorous and entertaining attack on waffle which everybody interested should read, George Orwell goes out of his way to stigmatise what he calls the *not un-* formation, which he would like to see laughed out of existence. He says in a footnote.

> One can cure oneself of the *not un-* formation by memorising this sentence: *A not unblack dog was chasing a not unsmall rabbit across a not ungreen field.*

Really? Orwell was an outstandingly silly as well as a very intelligent and observant man, and here I think he goes too far. He was right to have got fed up with the waffly reluctance to commit oneself enshrined in such phrases as *not unconnected with* and *a not unpromising development*, but surely wrong to miss the possible virtues as well as the more selfish advantages of an unwillingness to commit oneself. Further, whatever he may have thought or said, not every statement or opinion is a political one, and there is no evasion in writing, for instance, *the gaoler spoke to him not unkindly* in preference to *the gaoler spoke to him kindly*, which means something quite different. *Not un-* needs keeping an eye on, like much else, but there is no point in mechanically abolishing it, even if one could.

Nouns as verbs

The English language is friendly to the practice of using as verbs what until the other day were nouns only, and the dictionary is full of well-established verbs that started life in this way. Nevertheless, there are times when this sort of verb seems to be growing too fast for comfort, and one suspects that now may be such a time.

Nobody with any feeling for words can be glad at the arrival as verbs of *author* ('she has authored a dozen books'), *fund* ('how the award will be funded is not yet clear'), *guest* and *host* ('among those *guesting/hosting* the party was Mrs Joe Bloggs'), *target* ('gay bishop targeted'), or, according to report, *critique* ('to critique all aspects of life'). All these are easily avoidable blemishes. Yes, they may be quicker to say, but then cutting your arm off will reduce your weight faster and more irreversibly than any diet or exercise.

Number

(The grammatical term comprising, in English, singular and plural word-forms.)

The subject is hard for anybody not educated in it to understand. For instance, pick out the correct ones from the following catalogue and say how they resemble each other:

1. Violent crimes is a national growth-area.
2. Violent crime is many things, not one.
3. Violent crimes are a national growth-area.
4. Violent crime are many things, more than one.

Easy: the correct sentences above are 2 and 3. Perhaps not so easy: they resemble each other in that their respective verbs are of the same number as, or agree with, the subject of each sentence. And by the way, 1 and 4 resemble each other in that their respective verbs agree in their number with the complement of each sentence, the parts that come after *is* and *are*, not the subject. Laughably easy, both parts of this, for those readers who knew what grammatical number was before glancing at this article.

The emergent rule, that in each sentence the verb takes the number of the subject and never mind what comes after the verb, sounds easy enough to follow. Mistakes are sometimes made in sentences like the following:

> Close study of Nazi records, many of which are available to interested inquirers, especially if they carry letters introducing themselves, suggest dozens of conclusions.

After the event it is probably easy enough to spot the fact that *suggest* should be *suggests*. What threw the supposed writer off was first the sheer distance between the subject and its verb, and secondly the intervention of half a dozen plurals between the two and the presence of another couple just after the main verb. This sort of attraction is obviously the more likely the longer and more complicated the sentence, which is part of the argument for keeping one's own sentences short and straightforward.

The small but troublesome word *what* sometimes raises difficulties here, and to treat it as an unchanging singular solves most of them. *What I need is a stiff drink* is all right, but so is *What I need is twenty stiff drinks*, grammatically at least.

It would be a mistake to suppose that there is something disproportionate about using up all this space over the presence or absence of a single letter, as it commonly is. What is at stake is the comfort or discomfort of one's readers, and to suppose that this does not matter is a more serious mistake.

O

Oblivious

This once-useful word formerly meant something like *sadly forgetful*, as its Latin original suggests. A sentence like *Oblivious of his social position, he plunged into a life of gambling* shows it used in its original, precise meaning. Then, a hundred years ago or more, restless but lazy writers started using it as a posh synonym for merely *insensible*, as in *He stiffened in alarm, but the guard remained oblivious to [sic] his presence*. The difference is the substantial one between *not noticing* and *taking no notice of*.

As in other cases, all the writer who is careful with the words he uses can do is drop *oblivious* from his vocabulary and fall back on *forgetful*, *unaware* and the like.

Obscenity

The subject is adequately dealt with, I hope, under FOUR-LETTER WORDS, but I wanted to protest somewhere against the use of *obscene* and *obscenity* to refer to things that may be undesirable but are not 'grossly indecent, lewd' (*COD*). The full-sized *OED* gives as sense 1 of *obscene*:

> Offensive to the senses, or to taste or refinement; disgusting, repulsive, filthy, foul, abominable, loathsome. Now [1933] somewhat arch[aic].

The *Supplement to the Oxford English Dictionary* says under sense 1 of *obscene*:

> Delete 'Now somewhat arch.' and substitute 'Now [1982] restored to general use',

and proceeds to give citations from 1875, 1915, 1923 and 1936. Then we move to three from 1974, of which the first declares, not unexpectedly,

> Vietnam was the most obscene episode of the century,

and in the same year 'Broadmoor's forbidding buildings' are quoted as being 'obscenely overcrowded', after which many politically objectionable things were said to be *obscene*.

One hesitates to quarrel, even on a small scale, with the authority of the *OED*, but to my mind it goes wrong here. What we have seen, I would maintain, is much less the restoration to general use of a somewhat archaic sense than the impious and impudent hijacking or bagging of a word for sensationalist purposes. The kind of person who calls the events in Vietnam *obscene* is being irresponsible under the guise of moral shame. Dreadful things happen in the world all the time, and they are not made more objectionable by being misdescribed. These are not grossly indecent or lewd; in a word they are not what we have nowadays come to understand by *obscene*, however disgusting and depraved they may be.

OK, okay

The origin or origins of this English adjective, adverb, noun, verb and interjection are none of my concern, if my concern is supposed to be the correct or all-right usages of the language. For all that, one is sometimes expected to have a view of such matters, and so perhaps one should; I find it hard not to.

That does not mean to say any attention should be wasted on it. I have heard or seen in my time countless tales of the 'origin' of *OK* or *okay*, starting with the information in the old label on a bottle of O K Sauce to the effect that the Cherokee (or was it Choctaw?) for 'It is so' was *Hoke* or *Oke*. Quite possibly. I might very well have passed over the question in silence this time round, but yesterday my eye happened to fall on an 'explanation' new to me, viz. that the expression derives from the French words *Aux Cayes*, 'at the Keys', like Florida keys, from Spanish *cayo*, 'reef'. The words were supposedly stencilled on packages of new rum by Haitian freight-handlers to indicate that the contents had been made up 'at the Keys' and therefore included only the finest merchandise.

Again, quite possibly. To me, this 'explanation' is like the ones about *posh* being derived from the initials of 'port out, starboard home' and therefore to be given a cabin on the far side from the tropical sun; or *bloody* coming from 'blood' = parentage = [blue] blood = of first-rate quality = [bloody] good, etc. Or something. In other words, having been taken through the 'explanation' I feel no better, certainly no better informed, than before.

The *COD* is not the earliest authority to cite the initial letters of *oll korrect* as the 'origin' of *OK*. Pfui! Nobody really knows the story of *OK* or *posh* or *bloody* or a great deal else, and all we need is our existing knowledge of what the words mean and how they are used. The rest is small-talk and readers' letters in the *Daily Mail*.

On the third day

Christians know as certainly as they know anything that on the third day after his death on the cross Jesus rose again from the dead. Like many others I knew this myself at one time. Even while I knew it, however, another part of my mind was not to be prevented from seeing that Easter Day, Sunday, was only the *second* day after the day of crucifixion, Friday. This caused me no difficulty at that far-off time, and it cannot have been long afterwards that I abandoned all speculation about such matters.

The answer to the problem is, as usual, that there is no problem. The ancient world reckoned the passage of time inclusively, so that to every Roman yesterday was two days ago and tomorrow came along in two days' time. And any Sunday was the third day after the preceding Friday, whatever else might have been going on. This fact cannot have been generally known for some centuries, but I have never heard of any Christian who seems to have experienced difficulty in believing two apparently incompatible things at once. This would appear to point to a discreditable incuriosity about one of the fundamental articles of Christian faith.

Only

This little word has the property of straying from its logical position in a sentence or phrase, an eccentricity firmly entrenched in idiom and reinforced millions of times a day by English-speakers all over the world. No such person would say, for instance, 'Nelson seemed to lose his touch only when he fought on land,' instead of 'Nelson only seemed to lose his touch' etc. (In writing you might have to think again so as not to be taken as saying N. only *seemed* to, he didn't really.)

The 'misplacing' of *only*, like the split infinitive and other fancied lapses from verbal rectitude, inevitably draws the fire of parlour grammarians, 'those friends from whom the English language may well pray to be saved,' as Fowler calls them in this connection. His dislike of such people is so strong that it actually betrays him into a mixed metaphor when he says of them, 'they were ... slapping a strait waistcoat upon their mother tongue,' a lapse, but not a very sad one.

Onto

This form, rather dated now, will strike many readers as a would-be neat or smart or up-to-date version of *on to*, as if *into* were a neat etc. version of *in to*, which it is not. I have no great personal objection to *onto*, though I have found by experience that no one (not no-one) persistently using *onto* writes anything much worth reading. There seems to be a similar connection, or lack of one, between starting lines of verse with a lower-case letter and inability to write a worth-while (not worthwhile) poem.

Opine

There is not much of a case against this word, which means to hold or express an opinion and appears in general to be correctly used. Its attractions, I suppose, are that it remains for the moment a smart-looking synonym for *say*, and if what was said was adequately banal *opined* will draw attention to that, as in, for instance, 'He opined that the weather was seasonable.' This would appeal to writers who like to seem superior to what they report or describe. Indeed *opine*, though unfortunately rather short for the job, has something of the quality that made essayists of an earlier generation think it amusing to call a drunk man an intoxicated individual. That something no doubt resides in the Latinity/ formality of the word. When I add that, for whatever reasons, it has evidently become fashionable, handy for cheering up a lack-lustre diary para, I sense that there is a stronger case against *opine* than I thought when I started this article.

Optimistic

When a public figure says he is *optimistic* about the future of something, he chooses the word in preference to *hopeful* not only because *optimistic* is posher and longer but also because it seems more hopeful, rather as *hopefully* seems more hopeful than *I hope*. To be *optimistic* in what one may be tempted to call the true sense, certainly the original sense, is to hold a generally sanguine view of the universe or at least possess a cheerful temperament. I once heard on the radio an exchange between a journalist and a poet in which, perhaps unexpectedly, it was the journalist who asked the poet if he was optimistic (by nature, in the old sense), and the poet who apparently knew only of the newer sense. He answered the question by asking, in effect, 'What about?' Yes, he was a lousy poet too.

Orchestrate

A fashionable verb, meaning not much more than *organise* but implying that the user has a superior intelligence system: any fool can *organise* a conspiracy but you have to know a lot and work hard and deviously to *orchestrate* one. There might have been a valuable extra sense, derived from the original musical one, of setting out in full detail what had originally been no more than a mere undeveloped basis, but journalists can be relied on to steer confidently away from any such potentially interesting idea.

Other

In early use, *other* or its ancestor sometimes meant 'second', a sense retained in the modern expression *every other day*, meaning not 'every day except the one specified' but 'every second day'. This was perhaps not a common use, but it was evidently common enough to carve out a place in our ordinal numbers for the word *second*, a Latin-based intruder among the impeccably Teutonic *first, third, fourth, fifth*, etc. *Pace* the purists, *other* on its own, without suffixed *wise*, is a respectable English adverb and there is no objection to, for instance, the following: *He had no time to look at the document other than cursorily.*

Our mutual friend

Mutual is an indispensable but tricky word more easily understood than defined. An attempt at the latter might read, 'Felt or done by each of two towards the other,' as in *mutual liking, mutual destruction, mutual admiration society*, often a less fussy way of saying *reciprocal*. So far so good. The trouble comes when *mutual* is made to mean something like *shared* or *joint*, as notoriously in *our mutual friend*. (Here Dickens may or may not have meant to quote an ignorant character in the novel.) The usage and the famous phrase have passed into colloquial English, though not into mine. If we could say *our common friend* our troubles would be over, but in England a real grammatical solecism is preferable any day to a fancied social solecism, and the risk of seeming to mean that the friend is vulgar or lower class is too embarrassing to be faced.

Overstatement

The language of newspaper headlines inevitably overstates. They exist not to advertise the truth but to catch attention as shortly as possible. They do not tell us what is probably the case, that the Prime Minister was mildly vexed when Buggins let out some small confidence, they announce instead, PM FURY AT BUGGINS BETRAYAL. Similarly, a brief spasm of disquiet at a threat to the tranquillity of a Party conference becomes PANIC AS VIOLENCE LOOMS AT EAST-BOURNE. Most people are well aware of this and many allow for it.

What is perhaps less widely understood is the degree to which ordinary newspaper language (if I may so put it) seems to be pushing in the same direction of overstatement, sometimes by means of or via what Fowler would have called popularising a technicality, usually from that shadowy area where psychiatry and medicine intermingle. Thus people are no longer upset or confused or flustered by an unpleasant experience, they suffer a *trauma* or are *traumatised* by it. More briefly and inaccurately, they are not merely *shocked*, nor *suffering from shock*; they are said to be, or describe themselves as being, *in shock*. In the proper sense, that is pathologically, *shock* is a state of utter prostration following over-stimulation of nerves by sudden pain or violent emotion, and can result in death. It is many times removed from any reaction to what is usually described as a shocking experience.

Examples could be expanded. Until the other day, to *bemuse* someone was to reduce him to a condition of stupor, of morbid numbness and apathy; now, a transient state of mild perplexity is evidently deemed sufficient. In perhaps lighter vein, I saw some time ago that New York people were '*paranoid* – with reason – about rising crime'. In case anybody really is ignorant on the point, *paranoia* is a type of mental derangement marked by delusions of grandeur, persecution mania and other phenomena into which reason as we know it cannot enter. Some New Yorkers are no doubt uncommonly sensitive and intermittently emotional, but only very few can be truly paranoid in so objective a matter. Very likely sensitive and emotional was all that was meant, but the writer, in search of a more stylish and voguish word, was led via a popularised technicality into overstatement.

Paranoia and its derivatives may still not be beyond rescue, but earlier captures have gone for good. To mind-doctors and the like, *mania* may still be a type of mental derangement marked by excitement, hallucinations and violence, but to everyone else it denotes nothing more than an affection or admiration for something (bibliomania, anglomania). Less acute conditions are distorted in the course of popularisation, so an *inferiority complex* ceases to be a state of assertiveness or megalomania (there goes another) to compensate for suppressed feelings of inferiority and becomes merely and irrevocably those feelings themselves. I suppose we should think ourselves lucky that a *maniac* can still be a mad person and is not confined to indicating a lovable eccentric.

Owing to/due to

This is a perfect example of what it is an example of: a grammatical distinction that was once clear-cut and perhaps no longer is, but needs to be observed for reasons no longer purely grammatical.

Let me explain. Strictly, you may say or write, 'Owing to lack of interest, the carol service has been cancelled,' or equally well, 'The cancellation of the carol service is owing to lack of interest.' You may also say or write, 'The cancellation of the carol service is due to lack of interest,' but not 'Due to lack of interest, the carol service has been cancelled.'

I have investigated the origins of this rule, and nothing substantial or satisfactory emerges. It seems to be just a rule.

Which does not mean that it can safely or praiseworthily be ignored, and I must confess that to my pair of ears or organs of grammatical fitness the exclusion of *due to* as an introductory phrase is justified. Would you comfortably say or write, 'Due to his swarthy complexion, he escaped the anti-European riots'?' Here, and in general, when in doubt follow the rule. This one is worth following for its own sake, not just in deference to the fact that elderly powerful persons happen to know about it.

P

Pairs and snares

This is the heading Fowler gives his characteristically entertaining article on misleadingly similar pairs of words, similar usually through a common etymology. Here for once I suspect him of having inflated his list a little for show. While his warnings are always to be taken seriously, I feel that no more than four of his fifty or so listed pairs offer anything very perilous in the way of snares. I will try to deal with the surviving four.

1. *Alternate* and *alternative*. That would present no problem were it not for a chiefly American use of *alternate* and *alternative* in certain contexts, particularly in a science-fictional one. Here an imaginary world in which, say, the Reformation failed to take place and Roman Catholicism has become prevalent is likely to be called an alternate world. Simple enough if you keep your head.
2. *Compose* and *comprise*. Just to set it out, the various items on a list *compose*, constitute, make up that list, which is *composed* of those items; a list *comprises*, comprehends, includes the items, the list consists of them. Thus woodwind, brass, percussion and strings *compose* a full symphony orchestra; such an orchestra *comprises* woodwind, brass, percussion and strings. Worth getting straight.
3. *Derisive* and *derisory*. Journalists and others still busily confuse these two. *Derisive*=scoffing, as in a *derisive* yell, a yell of *derision*. *Derisory*=ridiculous, unworthy of serious

discussion, as in a *derisory* offer, a bid so low as to be *derisory*. Worth getting straight.

4. *Masterful* and *masterly*. Also often confused, especially by writing *masterful* when *masterly* is clearly intended. *Masterful*=wilful, domineering; *masterly*=immensely competent, befitting a master. Thus Mozart's operas can be said to be *masterly*. It seems somehow *important* to get this straight.

And a couple that have come up since Fowler's time:

5. *Baleful* and *baneful*. To write *baleful* when *baneful* is clearly intended has become very popular. The two words are easily confused, not only because of their close similarity but also because the ideas of pain and destruction are common to both, and both have an archaic/poetical ring to them. But *bale*=evil, woe, pain, while *bane*= poison, cause of ruin, thus a *baleful* glare but a *baneful* influence. Worth getting straight if possible.

6. *Complement(ary)* and *compliment(ary)*. Only a little effort is required to make the right choice here.

7. *Discreet* and *discrete*. The second word is newly fashionable and is quite often used instead of the first, perhaps by those who mistake *discrete* for a classy, up-to-the-minute spelling of *discreet*. I hope I need not say that in speech it is disCREET but DIScrete.

Panacea

Another once-useful word, whose original meaning was almost exactly *universal remedy*, *cure-all*. The prefix *pan*, meaning *all*, is well enough known, one would have thought, what with *pan-European* conferences, *Pan-American* aircraft, etc., but not everywhere, it seems. Quite recently, lazy and incurious writers began, irreversibly as always, to use the word when they meant nothing more than *remedy* or *cure*, as was shown by a new-fangled tautology, *universal panacea*. This forced careful writers to use *cure-all* when they meant that and *cure* when they meant that. The reader, in typical fashion, is left to puzzle over just what is meant on encountering *panacea*.

Parameter(s)

Parameter is a mathematical expression denoting a 'quantity constant in case considered, but varying in different cases' – far too technical and difficult for verbal novelty-hunters and seekers after poshness, who this time only wanted a newish word meaning 'limits', something not too far from *perimeters*, only different. How important it must have made leaders of this and that feel, to read that on behalf of their membership they had laid down the *parameters* of discussion. And still in use. I heard it on the radio only yesterday, and I was going to round off this article with a small song of triumph at the disappearance from the media of this repulsive word.

Parody, satire, comedy, irony, humour, wit

These words have areas of meaning that may overlap, and the words themselves may be intended in differing senses by different speakers. For all that, some agreement is advisable and may even be discerned here and there.

Parody. Best kept as a literary term denoting a piece that sets out to amuse by exaggerating stylistic and other qualities. I know only one such that has no amusing intention to be seen, 'The Hero' by Roger Woddis, which parodies a poem by Yeats as part of a devastating attack on terrorists, specifically those who carried out the Birmingham pub bombings of 21 November 1974. In most cases the purpose is not unkindly, though some critical strictures on the original can be detected in, for instance, C.S. Calverley's parody of Browning, 'The Cock and the Bull'. If used outside technical limits the term is necessarily vaguer, as when in his poem 'The Donkey' G.K. Chesterton calls the animal 'The devil's walking *parody*/On all four-footed things'. He might have done better with *travesty* but for its association with changes of costume.

Satire is amusing only incidentally, if at all, and has or used to have a moral intention, to expose vice and folly as a means of correcting them, in theory at least. Again the word is at its most precise in a literary context, referring to the works of the classical writers and Swift or Pope. In recent years almost any old TV show put together in a jeering or mocking or generally 'irreverent' spirit gets called satirical or a satire. The same thing happens to any reasonably diverting novel that treats of some particular environment, like an advertising agency or a school. In my opinion this is all mistaken. Let Anthony Powell put the point in the course of his remarks on Ronald Firbank. Powell describes 'an inept, not to say fatuous form of contemporary criticism to which Americans are peculiarly subject', and goes on:

> This lack of contact derives from an inability to distinguish between comedy and satire. When a comedian imitates a drunk man, he is not miming a tract against alcoholism. He is being funny. Mr Micawber is not a 'satire' against improvident officers of Marines. He is a great comic figure. Thus with Firbank. He was being funny about priests, and – dare one hint it? – about Negroes. [Written in 1970]

Comedy. Here, as already hinted, breadth and some vagueness of definition are called for. In literary terms the word continues to be more often applied to a work for the stage or broadcasting than to novels, though this distinction is being steadily eroded. There are historical connections with the portrayal of ordinary folk rather than grand personages, and in medieval times there was a requirement that the story of a comedy should begin in adversity and end prosperously (*The Divine Comedy*), but over the centuries the spirit of comedy, the comic muse, has come to require little but the intention to divert, to tickle, to cause to laugh. Attempts at a more particular distillate have been unsuccessful, as far as I am aware.

Irony. The non-literary use of the word *ironical* is dealt with under that heading. Almost separably, stylistic irony is well defined in *COD* as the 'expression of one's meaning by language of opposite or different tendency, esp. simulated adoption of another's point of view', before dramatic or tragic irony is defined as 'words having an inner esp. prophetic meaning for audience, unsuspected by speaker'. In the conversational sense, irony has something English about it, or so English critics have felt, but it is no more than one possible weapon among several in the armoury of the comic writer and is associated with no particular literary form.

Humour. This is no more definable than poetry, with which it has other affiliations. Humour speaks to the comic sense, whatever that is; one might as well just say it makes people laugh. Something more, perhaps, emerges from a comparison with wit, than which humour can be seen as blunter, broader, kinder, less verbal. To inquire further would be as unprofitable as trying to explain why fairs, the coconut-shy sort, have stayed popular over the centuries.

Wit. Like humour, this quality is much more easily recognisable when it appears than encompassed by a generalisation. Unlike humour, wit has a characteristic form of expression in the epigram or aphorism and a characteristic weapon or technique in the pun or play on words. Bits of it can be extracted and repeated without much loss. Wit needs no context. The word has a possibly misleading archaic sense. Applied to a man or woman it means somebody of mental ability, and in saying that great wits were sure to madness near allied Dryden meant chaps of great intelligence, not great after-dinner speakers. Yet an implication of intellectual liveliness remains in the modern use of the word.

Perceive, perception

To perceive something, or that something is so, used to mean simply to *take in* with the senses or the mind; you would *perceive* a tree on the horizon or the importance of heredity. The word is almost a synonym for *see*, except that a degree of effort or special ability is implied. But whatever you *perceived* was understood to be really there.

Then, in the earlier 1970s, a new meaning started creeping in. From then on what was perceived no longer had to be really there, it might be just the way you *saw* it, looked at it, *saw* not in the primary meaning of taking in reality but in the secondary meaning of taking a view of, e.g. *I see things differently now.* Nowadays journalists write of X's *perception of the Labour Party* when X might *see* the Labour Party as anything from a capitalist conspiracy to a gang of communists, while Y's *perception* might be entirely different and yet equally 'valid'.

When Samuel Johnson said to an acquaintance, 'Sir, I perceive you are a vile Whig,' he certainly did not mean to say anything as wishy-washy as that his uneven and temporary view of the chap took him to be some sort of vile Whig; he meant he now *knew* the other chap was a depraved supporter of parliament rather than crown, etc. As Johnson would have known, the Latin roots of *perceive* indicate that it meant to *grasp thoroughly*. Latin roots of English words are notoriously often bad guides to meaning, but not seldom, as here, they may remind the user of what the English word once unequivocally meant.

This user of *perceive* and *perception* will remain at best potential until further notice. The distinction between their traditional and contemporary meanings is quite substantial enough to deter me from ever running the risk of being thus misunderstood. Such is a common result of verbal innovation: instead of anything valuable, it causes either muddle or the departure of a once-useful word.

Pidgin Latin

In origin, French is a creolised Latin pidgin. In less abstruse terms, what we now know and have for centuries known as the French language is a simplified and corrupt form of Latin once current between Roman troops or colonists or traders on the one hand and the local peasantry on the other, a form of language eventually creolised, i.e. adopted as the one and only language of the locals. Spanish, Provençal, Catalan and others evolved along similar lines.

Like its sister languages, what became French contained at some stage versions of sundry words and constructions and equivalents, some perverted almost out of recognition: who for instance would guess that *avec* ('with') comes from *apud hoc*? Somehow Romanised Gauls put together a verb *aller* ('to go') out of ragged bits of at least three distinct Latin verbs, *vadere* meaning 'to hurry' (je *vais*), *ambulare* 'to walk' (nous *allons*, cf. English *amble*) and *ire* 'to go' (j'*irai*). One easily imagines dialogues between a scrounging legionary, perhaps a Vandal or a Parthian by origin, and a willing but benighted yokel.

LEGIONARY (in vile Latin) : I want water. Bring me water. *Aquam.*

YOKEL: Ugh?

L.: *Aquam*! Say *aquam*, you bloody fool. Go on – *aquam*.

Y.: O? (To be spelt *eau* when they get to the writing stage centuries later.)

L.: Bring it to the high cliff. The high cliff. *Altum*.

Y.: Ugh?

L.: *Altum*! Say *altum*, you bumpkin. Go on – *altum*.

Y.: O? (To be spelt *haut* when, etc.)

Latin left its mark even where the locals did not adopt a pidgin-Latin as their mother tongue. This is especially visible in place-names.

L.: Bring a dozen eggs to the place where the rivers join. *Confluentiam*.

Y.: Ugh?

L.: *Confluentiam*, you clodhopper.

Y.: Coblenz?

So with *Pfalz*, one syllable from the five of *palatinatam*. Etc.

We in what is now GB are not altogether free of this imputation.

L.: Our chaps are thinking of calling this place *Eboracum*. Go on, *say it*, you bog-trotter.

Y.: York?

These observations are intended not so much for home consumption as for that of anybody who may be in danger of forgetting that the language of Racine and Voltaire took its first steps not in any perfumed court or candle-lit cloister but in the lee of some rain-soaked dunghill. Should the subject come up, you have my permission to add that, although the lexical effect of Norman French on English was monumental, the structure of the latter is indigenous.

Pleasantry

A pleasantry is not a kind word or an amiable remark but a playful word or a joke, though often used nowadays to mean a pleasant bit of behaviour. The original sense derives from an archaic sense of *pleasant* meaning 'jocular, facetious, light-hearted, full of mirth'. When we read in the second book of Samuel that 'Saul and Jonathan were lovely and pleasant in their lives,' we are being told, not just that they were nice-looking and friendly, but something much more interesting and attractive, that their relationship was both affectionate and humorous.

Policy

Some of these entries are justifiable, if at all, chiefly because I had some remark to make and could find no better place to make it. This is one of those, although in its small way it offers an apposite moral.

You still hear people say 'Honesty is the best policy,' meaning no more than what the words will now bear, that fair dealing is the best general plan. No doubt, but perhaps not worth elevating to the status of an aphorism. Few can now be aware that what has become a bland near-platitude was once a disrespectful paradox meaning very nearly that honesty is the best trickery, and certainly that fair dealing will get you further than any clever stratagem. But that was when *policy* could be used to mean underhand behaviour, a sense the *OED* pronounced obsolete in 1933, its latest citation being dated 1849. It is more widely known that *politician* started life as a crafty planner or intriguer, a sense first recorded in 1588 and obsolete by the end of the eighteenth century.

When a piece of accurate cynicism or well-directed spite passes out of currency, something is lost.

Political words

This is not going to be an essay on such well-known slipperinesses as *democracy* and *freedom* but a short discourse on politically handy verbs and other expressions that are similarly adaptable. They may incidentally offend in philological ways but their primary offence is that they are attempts to gull the reader or hearer, to practise a verbal sleight of hand. What follow are examples only.

1. *Refute.* This word once had the useful meaning of proving falsity or error by argument and/or a recital of facts; it was not a mere synonym of *reject* or *rebut*. Then, some time in the 1960s, most likely while Harold Wilson was Prime Minister, it began to be used to mean *deny*, meaning really no more than it had always meant, a mere declaration that something was untrue. And yet, with the old basic sense of the word still hanging about in the public mind, it did sort of mean more than just *deny*, it implied too that there were or might be facts around that would back up the denial if they were produced.

Refute also carried a valuable suggestion of dignity, several cuts above the indignant protestations of a junta that their aims were not tyrannical and far superior to the captured criminal's denial of charges against him. No wonder that an American president said he categorically *refuted* the accusation that he had abused his powers, or that a local authority should *refute* without satisfactory argument the idea that their proposals were wasteful. The word is now unusable by any person of intelligence and taste.

2. Sorry, but this is a case too famous to be passed over in a work of the present sort. Unlike *refute*, *hopefully* in the sense of 'it is to be hoped (that)' has never been respectable. When someone says or writes, 'Hopefully, the plan will be in operation by the end of the year,' we know immediately that we are dealing with a dimwit at best. The most serious objection to the use of *hopefully* in a dangling position, often

signalled by a following comma, is not that it is not good English, though it is not, nor that it is a trendy usage, though it is, nor even that the thing remains obstinately afloat after many well-aimed salvoes of malediction, but that it is dishonest. In the example given, all that is really meant is, 'I/we hope the plan will be in operation by the end of the year,' or still less dishonestly, 'With luck, the plan,' etc., but the type who says or writes *hopefully* puts on a false show of nearly promising something while actually saying precious little. A favourite with politicians and even more with publishers.

3. *Up to.* This is admittedly not one word but two; nevertheless the two function as one. Used together, they behave with characteristic dishonesty. In a sentence like 'The plan will create up to fifty new jobs' an instant's reflection shows that the syntax leaves it open whether perhaps forty-eight new jobs or perhaps four new jobs may 'eventuate'. The reader or hearer is stranded in a condition of foggy optimism, half aware that an unspecified number of new jobs may be coming along while nothing has actually been pledged or even *said*, a highly satisfactory condition for an elector to be in from the point of view of somebody standing for election.

Popular etymology

This means, not a much-liked branch of linguistic science, but the erroneous rephrasing of an unfamiliar expression as one more familiar; folk etymology is another name for the same thing. An early supposed example substituted the odd but non-foreign *sparrowgrass* for the Latin or Greek *asparagus*. As both food and word grew less unexpected, so *sparrowgrass* faded from sight. A more durable instance is afforded by *varicose* as in veins, meaning dilated in a special way. Hundreds of mostly elderly people are afflicted by varicose veins for every one who has the faintest idea of the history of the term. No wonder popular etymology flourishes here, and the old ladies who suffer, or describe their friends as suffering, from *various* veins or, less familiarly, from *very close* veins must be numbered in almost as many hundreds. Or they used to be. A more up-to-date popular etymology is a *quick* Lorraine, recently offered me as a snack lunch as I got myself ready to dash off somewhere.

Other notorious cases include *Jerusalem* artichoke and *hiccough*. The artichoke matter is highly learned, showing that not all such etymologies are associated with illiteracy. *Jerusalem* in this phrase is a corruption of an ultimately Italian original, *girasole* or gyrate-sun, sun-follower, sunflower, of which this artichoke is a species with edible roots. *Hiccough* is all home-grown, an attempt to normalise and domesticate the unEnglish-looking *hiccup*, earlier *hicket*, which sounds much more like an actual hiccup than *hiccup* does. As anyone knows who has had an attack of hiccups, the performance does not in the least resemble a series of coughs, but *cough* is a decent God-fearing English word with roots in Old English. This desire for a kind of linguistic respectability, the look if not the fact of genuineness, guaranteed the survival of *belfry*, which started life in the twelfth century as *berefreid*, became *berfrey* and *barfrey* and then quite abruptly in the fifteenth century turned into *belfry*, which everyone knows is the abode of bells, and so it has comfortably remained ever since.

The story of *avocado* is more remarkable and also exotic (=with foreign origins). Our starting-point is the word *ahuacatl*, the Aztec term for the pear-shaped tropical fruit. It takes some finding out, but evidently *ahuacatl* in non-frugivorous contexts means testicle, not much of a metaphor unless a monorchid scrotum and a pear of the Florida (Gulf of Mexico) rather than the California variety are visualised, and even then . . . Anyway, *ahuacatl* as it stood would clearly not do for the sixteenth-century Spanish invaders of Mexico. The *tl* termination had to go, as it went in *chocolatl* and *tomatl*, and the final answer was rather surprisingly *avocado*, 'lawyer'. *Avocado* in its turn would not do at first for the English, who took things through another stage of popular etymology, and until not so long ago one ate an *alligator* pear, what with the exotic and tropical connotations and the sometimes knobbly skin a good deal more appropriate than anything to do with lawyers. But as we all know, in the end *avocado* triumphed, helped perhaps by looking foreign on the menu but at the same time being easy to say. Some British eaters call it *advocado* to this day just to be on the safe side.

I have said that there is no necessary link between popular etymology and illiteracy; nevertheless the one flourishes where the other is widespread, and Jamaica is or was a place of high illiteracy and plenty of things with odd or learned names like exotic plants. One of the more outlandish examples is the plant known popularly as *simple-bible* or *single-bible*, botanically as *supervivium*, with of course its first I a long vowel. The tree *poinciana*, more understandably perhaps, became *Fancy Anna*. Place-names, or names for topographical features, are especially suitable to popular-etymology treatment. My favourite in all this field is the local name for an unusually deep body of water on the island, the *Wag Water*. It seems as certain as such things ever are that this name is a corruption of the Spanish *agua alta*, 'deep water'. How satisfying that the original word for 'water' changes into something quite arbitrary and the word meaning 'high' becomes *water*. Sound-change comes in here: at the time the 'translation' was made *water* must have been pronounced not as it is now, something like *wawter*, but as it still was in the earlier nineteenth century, something like *watter*, to rhyme with *flatter*. In 1820 or thereabouts Byron wrote:

> I say, the future is a serious matter:
> So now – for God's sake, hock and soda-water!

which requires *water* to be pronounced as described if the rhyme is to be true.

If any reader still needs reassurance, let me be quite emphatic that the Romans too had their popular etymologies. One of them has given us the English word *posthumous*, which derives ultimately from classical Latin *postumus*, meaning 'last', connected with *post*, meaning 'after', often given to a last-and-no-mistake son, one born after the death of his father. Somebody in the Dark Ages, mindful of the Latin word *humus*, meaning 'earth' or 'ground' and so no doubt suggesting thoughts of burial, slipped in an H that had no business to be there.

Finally, there are false popular etymologies only a few streets away, very common for some reason with the names of pubs. The Elephant and Castle, one of the four London pubs supposed to have given its name to a district, is often said to have been The Infanta of Castile. No; it had a sign showing an elephant with a castle (contemporary term for a howdah) on its back. Then there was The Goat and Compasses, alias God Encompasseth Us. No comment, except that it sounds a bit unlike the first place you would call at for a reviving glass.

Popular horrors

These expressions are not worth articles to themselves. Mentioning them here will have to do.

feedback. Has a precise use in mechanics and electronics but is pissily and pretentiously used by psychologists and others to mean nothing more than 'comment' or 'response' (as from a 'patient').

in-depth. No committee these days would dream of 'funding' a survey or analysis that was not said to be an *in-depth* survey etc. A mere *deep* one draws few dollars.

in terms of. A great anytime thought-saver. To be avoided even in correct use, for instance speaking of expressing feet and inches in terms of metres and centimetres. A trustworthy shibboleth, like *the arts*, in that nobody who uses it in ordinary conversation without some sort of jeer or sneer is to be trusted.

ongoing (situation). As above. Anything wrong with *present* or *current*?

or whatever. Try to avoid this in speech. Never write it.

-type. This, as in *guerrilla-type war*, is a lazy time-saver, but is not actually criminal unless *situation* follows it, as in *Vietnam-type situation.*

Popular misspellings

Any fool can misspell, and many do in a sporadic, random, innocent sort of way, but a few words evidently cause widespread difficulty, not necessarily for any apparent reason. Even quite good people, for instance, sometimes write *supercede* instead of the correct *supersede*, obviously muddled by the nearby presence of *concede*, *intercede*, etc., but why so many, good and bad, should write that something is a great *suprise* causes me some mild surprise as well as puzzlement. Perhaps pronunciation is a guide: no comparable English word beginning with *sur-* (or *ser-* or *sir-*) swallows its first syllable in that way, and *suppose* in childish or illiterate speech is often heard and printed as *s'pose*, though never so spelt.

Other popular misspellings, with some possible explanations, include:

accommodate. Is often spelt with only one M. Due to laziness.

develop with an extra E stuck on the end. Attraction from *envelope.*

gutteral for *guttural.* Due to ignorance, plus possibly some unconscious xenophobia.

idiosyncracy like a form of government. Confusion with *democracy* etc.

practice/practise. Laziness, plus perhaps some US influence.

principal/principle. Laziness.

seperate instead of *separate.* I have no idea why. Influence from *sever?*

Like all good spellers, I have never experienced any real difficulty here. I admit to some slight recent hesitation over *instal, instalment* and *instil.* Should the L be doubled? No, only in America. To plead American influence to defend an English mistake is only half a defence.

I have not listed all popular misspellings, but there are not many more. Their general paucity is a strong recommendation of the English orthographical system. There must be a lot to be said for what comes naturally to nearly everyone nearly all the time.

Power of words

Anyone who doubts the power of words should consider the importance often attached to them by reasonable people. Or such a person might take a look at Ulster, where a few words are busily and effectively fighting on the side of those who want the whole of Ireland to be governed by Dublin.

The United Kingdom of Great Britain and Northern Ireland is the cumbersome full name of our country, of that part of the world that we are citizens of. Not surprisingly, no convenient collective name for those citizens suggest itself, as for instance *Canadians* describes citizens of Canada or *Italians* those of Italy. It is for this reason among others that the word *British* has become the accepted description of our citizens. This works all right most of the time even though it is inaccurate, taking no account of the one and a half million or so who live in Northern Ireland.

When *British* becomes the name for citizens of the UK, when our army becomes known as the *British* army instead of what it actually is, the army of the UK, injustice is unconsciously done those people and the many among them who serve in our armed forces. No doubt they have grown used to that. What they may not have got used to so readily is not being thought of as citizens of that awkward entity, the United Kingdom.

An English friend said to me recently of the Irish problem, 'I think we should get out,' a very popular and pissy view. By 'we' he clearly meant the British, reminding me of an ignorant and admirably clear-cut American slogan, 'England get out of Ireland'. To talk in this strain is only possible for those who have never started thinking. *Of course* one country should get out of, cease interfering with, another; the trouble is that what is being petitioned for here is not that but the expulsion of part of a country (Northern Ireland) by that country as a whole (the United Kingdom of Great Britain and Northern Ireland).

There are obviously several reasons for the trouble in and about Northern Ireland, but the use of a few words is among the most intractable.

Predictable

The Leader of the Opposition reacted with predictable indignation to an accusation that he was the paid employee of a foreign Power.

This is a parody, to be sure, but not a very far-fetched one. Every day, people are shown to be reacting in ways so fully predictable that one may wonder what the word is doing in that context. What it is usually doing, of course, apart from lending tone, is subtly suggesting that (a) the commentator is too intelligent and well informed ever to be surprised by anything, and (b) the bit of conduct mentioned was insincere, perhaps even rehearsed in advance. All this is a substantial return for a small outlay, cheap at the price, so cheap indeed that the word might be given a rest.

Preposition at end of sentence

This is one of those fancied prohibitions (compare SPLIT INFINITIVE) dear to ignorant snobs. In this case they should be disregarded, and they mostly are, though the occasional stylistic derangement may suggest that a writer here and there still feels its force. It is natural and harmless in English to use a preposition to end a sentence with. As Fowler famously observed, 'The power of saying ... *People worth talking to* instead of *People with whom it is worth while to talk* is not one to be lightly surrendered.' This time idiom and common sense have triumphed over obscurantism.

Pristine

This is not a new word meaning 'spotlessly clean' but an old word (first recorded 1534) meaning 'original, ancient, primitive'. I suppose there is enough overlap of the two meanings, via references like 'a shirt restored to its pristine splendour', to explain something of how the old word was taken up as an attractive novelty. Usable by those who like attractive novelties even when they only seem to be novelties.

Pronunciation and accent

These are two ways of describing how we speak. My attempt to differentiate them here is meant not as the drawing of a sharp or final distinction but just a matter of convenience. So somebody may speak in a way that strikes his hearers as markedly individual, but for all that everyone's *accent* is a general thing that depends roughly on a speaker's place of birth, upbringing, education and subsequent environment, whereas *pronunciation* is a question of how individual words are spoken. Therefore it may make sense to talk of an American accent or a Suffolk accent or a public-school accent, and even to think of one as 'better' or 'worse' than another overall, but one pronunciation of a given word will be considered 'correct' and another 'incorrect'. It has become respectable to say so only in the quite recent past. See RECEIVED PRONUNCIATION.

For practical purposes, an *accent* is chiefly a matter of how vowels and suchlike are said, an obvious example being the 'Northern' or 'North-country' U in words like *bug* and *bud*; *pronunciation* often concerns the stressing in a given word, so that the correct way to pronounce *formidable* is with the stress on the first syllable and to put it anywhere else is incorrect.

Pronunciation as it now is

It may be deplorable, or at least seem old-fashioned to some, to talk of correct and incorrect pronunciation, but surely most of those who refer to or otherwise read a treatise on our language are looking for guidance rather than mere description, not least in the present category. They want to be told not what their neighbours or the educated or the half-educated or the vulgar or scholars say or avoid, but what they themselves should and should not say, what is correct and what incorrect. In 1926, Fowler found it sufficiently easy to instruct readers of *Modern English Usage* that:

> While we are entitled to display a certain fastidious precision in our saying of words that only the educated use, we deserve not praise but censure if we decline to accept the popular pronunciation of popular words ... Pronounce as your neighbours do, not better. For words in general use, your neighbour is the general public.

That view could only have been advanced when the division between educated pronunciation and popular pronunciation was more rigid than it is today, and perhaps by somebody whose neighbours lived next door in a college quadrangle rather than in a housing estate. Further, the imagined spectacle of Fowler in his talk nimbly leaping across that division, and a moment later as nimbly back again, causes me some uneasiness. I am not quite saying that in the passage quoted his chief intention was to vindicate his usual approach to linguistic problems. He was certainly doing more there than justifying his inclination to run with the liberal hare and hunt with the conservative hounds, but he was doing that.

Today, too, Fowler might have had to recognise that the 'general public' often use words that in his time only the educated would have used, and more importantly that that 1990s general public no longer learn their pronunciation chiefly from the practice of their elders and contemporaries but from other sources. The most important of these other sources is broadcasting, in a wide sense of that term. I intend not only what reaches us by television and sound radio, though it is predominant, but also film, the stage and various analogues and derivatives.

Pronunciation as they broadcast it

Young broadcasting performers, prominent performers, regular performers exercise a powerful influence on how the rest of us speak, an influence more immediate than that of courtiers, ecclesiastics, academics or any other dominant group of the past. Modern broadcasters do not of course speak with one voice, but by listening to them it is an easy matter to form an image of how the pronunciation of our language may be changing, perhaps irreversibly.

When one of us today hears a recording or sound-track of speech from before the last war, it sounds old-fashioned in several ways that have nothing to do with reproduction systems. In particular, the pronunciation of several easily differentiated vowel-sounds seems not to be as it was. To particularise further, the pronunciation of what used to be the short A (as in *bat*), the short E (as in *bet*) and the long vowel or diphthong AR or AIR (as in *bare*) is changing to something different, as follows:

i) The sound of short A is now close to what used to be short U (as in *but*). A broadcaster now seems to talk about 'the impuct of blucks' attucks on other blucks' in parts of Africa.

ii) The sound of short E is now close to what used to be short A. A broadcaster now seems to talk about 'lass attantion in the Prass' paid to something-or-other.

iii) The sound of AIR is also not what it used to be, but the change is more difficult to pin down without recourse to phonetic symbols. Here goes anyway. If in pre-war times a speaker talked about *air* or *bare*, the diphthong used consisted of an E-sound blended into a U-sound or something close to it. If a modern broadcaster talks about *air* or *bare*, she (see next section) uses a pure or near-pure A-sound of longer duration than the vowel once generally heard in words like *bat*. Try saying *bat* slowly without the final T and you may well produce a sound very like the trendy pronunciation of *bare*.

Anybody who finds parts of the foregoing abstruse can at once recognise what I mean by turning on the wireless, now often known under American influence as the radio. As I write (in 1994), as good an example as any is the speech of Classic FM, or Clussic Aff-Am in its own manner of speaking. Further pronunciation-trends to be found there and elsewhere include saying *-sheer* for *-shire* in names of counties (*Northamptonsheer* for old *-shub*) and a colouring of an E-vowel in short U-sounds (*sebmarine*, *hennyseckle*). This latter sound was once current among would-be posh speakers from the north-east of England, but shows recent signs of settling down as part of the generic sub-standard RP to be heard among radio news-readers. Another shibboleth is provided by the pronunciation of *one* more or less as *wan* (rhyming with *don*) in Northern fashion. There are further examples of the influence of broadcasting and broadcasters.

Pronunciation: he-she

For an essentially modern broadcaster (see last section) I would prefer to read *she* chiefly because the new sounds were first heard in public from young women, especially actresses of the 1940s, who perhaps felt that the old sounds helped to create a vaguely superior, scolding, finicky effect out of place in the then new Britain. See *Language Made Plain*, by Anthony Burgess, who was among the first to notice the new sounds. To this pair of ears, the old sounds do indeed seem a bit finicky, etc., in comparison, but at least they never seem gushing or girlish.

Pronunciation in general

Spelling-pronunciation, the tendency to allow or encourage
the way a word is spelt to influence the way it is spoken,
must be as old as the first attempts to commit speech-sounds
to paper. In English at least it is traceably very old. Evidence
from such sources as diaries and personal letters suggests
that, as always, men and women in the past spoke less
carefully and correctly in ordinary domestic dealings than
on formal occasions. Their practice in putting words on
paper was, as might be expected, generally similar. So when
we read, in a letter between friends, *Ile sen you an unnerd
poun*, we can guess that this closely follows the sounds of
actual informal talk, though we can be pretty sure too that
the sounds of formal, best-behaviour discourse would be
more closely represented by, *I'll send you a hundred pounds*.

Not very sure, however. If I may digress for a moment,
the way we now say *hundred* might well be the result of a
modern spelling-pronunciation, an opinion supported by
such evidence as the words *blundered, thundered* and *wondered*
offered as rhymes to *hundred* by the educated and fastidious
Tennyson ('The Charge of the Light Brigade', 1854) and
by the fact that older rustic speakers said something like
hunnerd within living memory. Perhaps some still do. I will
add here that the dropping of the final D in vocables like
sen and *poun* is paralleled by the occurrence in pre-war blues
lyrics of forms like *han* for *hand* and *mine* for *mind*.

Spelling-pronunciation (to resume) was greatly boosted
by the educational reforms of the nineteenth century, which
made it socially more difficult to speak like an illiterate
person. So the traditional *weskit* was firmly pushed out by
waistcoat, the monosyllabic *tords* yielded to the dissyllable
towards (though not in America), *perhaps* replaced the juvenile *praps* and the likely adult version *per'aps*, and the H
began to be sounded as never before in words like *hotel* and
humour. I conjecture too that during this period words hard

to pronounce 'properly', like *secretary* and *recognise*, lost their old pronunciations of *seckatry* or *seckaterry* and *reckanise* except among the 'lazy', the 'vulgar' and the 'uneducated'. What about *deteriate*?

The post-1945 educational 'reforms' (inverted commas denoting sarcasm are hard to avoid in the present context) made people more anxious than ever before to show that they were literate, i.e. able to read. Spelling-pronunciation entered its heyday and what had perhaps been heard only now and then became general and normal.

In 1926 Fowler could cover the subject in less than a column. He recommended that 'no effort should be made to sound the T in the large classes of words ending in -*sten* . . . and -*stle* . . . , nor in *often, soften, ostler, nestling, waistcoat* [of COURSE], *postpone* [less expected]. But some good people,' he continued with a show of leniency, 'afraid they may be suspected of not knowing how to spell, say the t in self-defence.' He might have added *chestnut* and *Christmas* to his list.

Fowler also went on to give a handful of samples of the many words 'whose spelling and ordinary pronunciation do not correspond, but with which mistaken attempts are made to restore the supposed true sound'. His first two samples are *clothes* and *forehead*, and I admit that I should rather like to be able to say *close* but from fear of being misunderstood do not dare, and that I unconsciously said *forrid* until the sincere incomprehension of a lecture-class in the 1950s brought me round to *fawhed* and to hell with Longfellow's little girl. (But see below.) So it goes with linguistic change: the aim of language is to ensure that the speaker is understood, and all ideas of correctness or authenticity must be subordinate to it.

One's readiness to embrace the last belief may suffer some weakening when the question turns to another pronunciational phenomenon, what might be called the intrusive H. 'In *Hunt has hurt his head*,' says Fowler, 'it is nearly as bad to sound the h of *has* and *his* as not to sound that of *Hunt* and *hurt* and *head*.' Seventy years after *MEU*, some observers might want to amend this to read, in part, 'far worse . . . than'. To pronounce those five words with no Hs at all is a mere piece of illiteracy or vulgarity, venial offences compared with the vices inherent in pronouncing all five Hs. The 5-H version may be judged slightly superior in point of intelligibility, but not by nearly enough to balance its appalling affectation and pedantry, indeed vulgarity of a less appealing sort than that of any zero-H version. And yet, all over the kingdom, real people, not just actors and actresses, are saying, '*H*is tie suits *h*im' and '*H*er dress fits *h*er' simply to show their hearers that they know an H when they see one. The old usage was that in ordinary talk little words like *has* and *his* and *her* and *he* had their Hs sounded only to mark emphasis: '*he*'s gone [but she's still here]' as against ''e's gone [without leaving an address]' – so went the rule, none the less a rule for going unmentioned, being taken for granted, and like many rules of language easier to understand than to explain.

'For a particular affectedly refined pronunciation,' writes Fowler, 'see GIRL.' It may be disappointing to some that, when they duly see GIRL, they find only a short note on how to and how not to pronounce that word, so that it 'rhymes with *curl*, *whirl* and *pearl*, with the first syllable of *early*, not of *fairly* . . .' Here I can wheel forward my Longfellow quatrain, which runs:

> There was a little girl and she had a little curl
> Right in the middle of her forehead,
> And when she was good she was very very good,
> but when she was bad she was horrid.

Nothing wrong with that, though unfortunately Fowler goes on, 'But a pronunciation gairl, not very easily distinguished from gal, is much affected by persons who aim at pecular refinement,' etc. Experience shows the danger of assuming that Fowler was ever unaware of anything, and perhaps the date is wrong for his apparent unawareness that the *gal* pronunciation is American rather than British, as in *Somebody Stole My Gal* et passim. And in any case the pronunciation he means to censure is surely *gel*, not *gal*, as in the speech of many born later than Fowler (b. 1858), and he also seems unaware of evidence that *gurl* was once a spelling-pronunciation, as in Max Beerbohm's caption to his caricature of Kipling (1896). But this is another digression.

Even at his best and most prophetic, one of Fowler's generation could never have foreseen the extent to which spelling-pronunciation, through the medium of a then undeveloped technology, would come to dominate our speech-habits. Except when delivering a news bulletin or the like, a broadcaster is not speaking in public in any close sense, but such a person must nevertheless be aware that untold thousands of people are or may be listening and anyway has some sort of duty to be (i) clearly heard and (ii) understood by as many listeners as possible whatever their own speech-habits. Once upon a time RP took care of any stragglers, but the world has moved on since then. It is no wonder if the result is a more precisely articulated mode of utterance than ordinary talk, a clarity of enunciation that will involve giving every syllable something like the value it has on the page, in fact liable to pronounce words as they are spelt. And several sorts of pressures will make it hard not to follow that example in one's own speech.

One obvious place to look for examples is in the pronunciation of those proper names which traditionally were not spoken as spelt. Among those no longer pronounced traditionally are Blount (formerly *Blunt*), Bohun (*Boon*), Cirencester (*Sissiter*), Coke (*Cook*), Daventry (*Daintry*), Hepburn (*Hebbun*), Ker and Kerr (*Kar*), Marylebone (*Maribun*), Pontefract (*Pumfrit*), St John (*Sinjun*), Waldegrave (*Wargrave*) and

Woburn (*Woobun*). It is probably true that a righteously egalitarian, who-does-he-think-he-is (to call himself Chumley when he spells his name *Cholmondeley*) spirit is also at work here.

These days we are pestered by something far more various, widespread and noticeable. The change is in the direction of pronouncing unstressed syllables with their full value, especially though not exclusively in unfamiliar or new words – I write 'in the direction of' because this is a tendency not yet completed. For instance, when I was young there was a contraceptive thing called a *condom*, pronounced *cond'm*; now, the evidently same thing is a *con-dom*, with a fully rounded second syllable. A year or two earlier I had been fond of a sweetmeat called a *caramel*, pronounced like *camel* with a brief extra syllable in the middle; it's a *caramell* now. As a sterling moderniser of Fowler's original has noted, *fortune* and *picture*, which used to be pronounced *forchoon* and *pickcher*, are now said as they are spelt, and *regiment* and *medicine* are usually spoken as trisyllables. *My* and *your* used to be fully pronounced only when emphatic, as in 'Well, it's not *my* hat [, it must be yours].' Otherwise, it was *muh* or *m'* as in *m'lud*, *m'tutor*: 'I've left *m'hat* behind.' Now we get the full treatment every time.

Proper names cop it too. There was a boy at school called *Ballard*, pronounced like *ballad*, rhyming with *salad*, by one of the masters, an elderly chap born probably in the 1870s. The boy himself called it *Ballahd*, like the rest of us, and of course the eminent writer of today is universally known as J.G. *Ballahd*, and jolly good luck to him. Also in those early years of mine there was a composer called Edward *Elgar*, second syllable like that of *sugar*; for a long time now the man has been *Elgah*. Well, unless his name gets its full value every time we might not all understand that it was he who wrote the Introduction and Allegro for string quartet and string orchestra. Foreign or foreign-looking names suffer from being sort of Europeanised, so we hear about the oratorio Judas *Maccabayus* and the overture *Layonora* no. 3, say.

The tendency to pedantically accurate pronunciation has been reinforced by the employment of broadcasters born outside the traditional RP area of south-eastern England. West-country speakers, like Irish and most Americans, were brought up to pronounce the R in words like *bard* and *bird*, north-country ones to give full value to words like *consider* and *perceive*. Such habits provide some of the hearable evidence of an inclination to speak in a way perceptibly different from oldsters and snobs. And anybody who feels that the old speech-habits are too firmly entrenched should take discomfort from my having heard, three or four times recently, one or other broadcaster pronounce the words *says* and *said* as *saize* and *sehd*, to rhyme with *stays* and *staid*. Most things are never meant, as Philip Larkin wrote, and we all know that a thing does not have to be meant by anyone in order to happen.

Fowler is a marvellous writer with among other gifts an inquisitive and accurate ear for speech-sounds, but in one regard he had it easier than his successors. The contents of a printed page will last at least as long as that page; a spoken enormity comes and goes in a flash without record. But perhaps I am alone in feeling we have among us a small and not very dangerous monster that is nevertheless hard to keep in check. I am less likely to be alone in thinking that educated people mispronounce words more than they used to.

On the whole, it seems that positive guidance or direction of broadcasters' speech is attempted in only a few cases, of which *-sheer* for *-shire* is presumably one. Others include the saying of 'one hundred' in full every time that quantity is mentioned, occasionally producing mini-nonsenses like 'a one hundred times over', and a more mysterious ruling that calls for an interval before penultimate or antepenultimate *and*. This quite often produces less trifling nonsenses like 'showers in midland [voice falls and a brief pause follows, as at the end of a sentence] And northern districts'. But these are easily detectable, and nothing more detailed or outrageous is to be heard, so for instance we are spared attempts to make six syllables of *extraordinary* or pronounce *England*, *English*, etc., according to the spelling.

I end this section with a brief polemic on the spread of the glottal stop. This is a kind of consonant or consonant-substitute that may take some explaining to the uninitiated. The linguistician Leonard Bloomfield defines it as a slight catch in the throat; a speaker of German uses it before every word that begins with a vowel, as before the second and third word in *Deutschland über alles*; in old-fashioned cockney and Glaswegian speech it comes in the middle of words like *letter* (*le'er*) and *button* (*bu'on*), generally doing duty for medial double T; it is a small puff of breath from the top of the windpipe. There.

I first heard the glottal stop in standard English speech in 1946, though it can be traced back to American broadcasting in the 1930s. The greater historical closeness to German of American speech compared with British is perhaps relevant here and helps to justify my mention of *Deutschland über alles*. The glottal stop would have recommended itself to some speakers as a handy way of escaping the temptation of an intrusive R in phrases like *law and order*. Whatever the exact reason or reasons, the new consonant-substitute soon spread all over the place among broadcasters and others. It was apt to pop up before any initial vowel anywhere, so that people started speaking not of the *IRA*, but of the `*I* `*R* `*A* with a glottal stop before each letter. I have even heard it used in the middle of a word, like *fore* `*arm*, and, once, Queen *Juli* `*ana* of the Netherlands. `*Our* Father, which `*art* in heaven . . . for `*ever* and `*ever*, `*amen*.

I object to this shopworn novelty in the first place as a German noise, while *lawr and order*, however unpleasant to some ears, is a British noise. More reasonably, perhaps, unnecessary glottal stopping seems an example of headlong pedantry, especially when associated, as it so often is, with affectations like sounding all one's Hs regardless of emphasis. English managed without such trumpery for hundreds of years. May it go on doing so.

Protagonist

In its time, this word has meant or been made or taken to mean at least four different things: the one and only chief actor in a stage production, the one and only central figure in a political or other awkward situation, one among several figures in an awkward situation, and the proponent or champion of a particular cause or view. The battle to determine the true or accepted meaning of the word was first joined perhaps a century ago and probably still rages in scattered common-rooms and libraries.

My advice is never to say or write *protagonist* yourself, thereby avoiding any possible misunderstanding or obloquy on the point. If you mean a central figure, say *central figure*, if you mean a proponent or champion, say *proponent* or *champion*. To abandon what was once a perfectly good, unambiguous word is no doubt to concede a small defeat, but life is short.

Psychotic

It is all right to say many things in conversation, including a lot of exaggerated and intemperate things. Thus to say *she literally drives me mad* is all right, but to put it on paper, to have it published is not, unless you mean *mad* literally and *literally* literally as well. *Psychotic* is one of the words you may say and welcome, but write only after due deliberation. The word *psychotic*, in print, means suffering from a severe mental derangement involving the whole personality, so of course you only write it if you are prepared to stand by it.

It would have been unnecessary to sound such a warning if it were not for the increasing influence of television and radio, which blur the distinction between the spoken and the written word. Broadcasting encourages people to *say* in talk what they would very likely not *write* and so only fleetingly and partially *mean*, but may nevertheless be faithfully preserved and if thought to be damaging to another may legally be quotable in an action not for slander but for libel. Not any longer is a word no sooner spoken than lost.

Puns

Fowler writes:

> The assumption that puns are *per se* contemptible, betrayed by the habit of describing every pun not as *a pun*, but as *a bad pun* or *a feeble pun*, is a sign at once of sheepish docility and desire to seem superior. Puns are good, bad, and indifferent, and only those who lack the wit to make them are unaware of the fact.

One would not want to alter a word of that, except possibly to replace *sheepish* with *sheeplike*. A codicil might be added, however, along the lines of there being places like newspaper headlines where puns may be thought to cluster too thick. See HEADLINE ENGLISH.

Q

Question-mark

No problem here, one might have thought, and certainly there is none while writers can tell the difference between a direct question (e.g. *Who are you?*) and an indirect question (e.g. *Ask him who he is* or *Tell me who he is*). Direct questions are followed by a question mark; indirect questions are not. Nothing easier, one would have thought. Alas, if one did one would have been wrong.

Plenty of direct questions are regularly ended with a full stop on the correspondence pages of newspapers. The writer kicks off by asking, *May I crave the hospitality of your columns* in order to right some piffling injustice or other, and by the time he has got to the end of his first dose of verbal Mogadon he has succumbed to it himself or simply forgotten how he started; anyway, he ends it with a full stop. To do so not only sends the interested reader, if there is one, back to the start to check that the fellow did at any rate start to ask a direct question, it also carries the disagreeable and perhaps truthful suggestion that the writer thinks a request from the likes of him is probably a needless politeness to the likes of the editor.

Even quite short direct questions are liable to be left without a question-mark if they are information questions (e.g. *What's on telly?*) as opposed to yes-or-no questions (e.g. *Anything good on telly?*). The oral link remains strong even when the writer never so much as subvocalises what he writes, and what he writes is apt to be, say, *When did you last change your car* full stop; he has 'heard' the speaking voice dip a little at the end of asking that information question, like somebody making a statement, and he knows well enough that statements are followed by full stops. (If his question is a yes-or-no question, with the voice 'heard' to lift at the end, he will put in a question-mark and write, say, *Would you like a new car free?*)

Question-marks are sometimes mistakenly put at the end of indirect questions if the writer feels specially interrogative and wants to remind his reader that the question he asks deserves an answer, or perhaps he is just carried away by herd-instinct. So he writes, *I wonder how many lunatics are actually living in the community?* and feels a sense of duty done. Nine times out of ten a sentence that opens with *I wonder* ends with an unwarranted question-mark.

In colloquial prose, or in dialogue where a speaker's tones and inflections may be more or less closely reproduced, these rules can be relaxed.

Quixotic

This misuse is uncommon, but it attracts attention by its very singularity. Traditionally, and still usually, *quixotic* means 'like Don Quixote in Cervantes' novel, i.e. characterised by lofty but impracticable ideals, indifferent to material advancement in comparison with honour and truth.' I cannot discover what has made the word sometimes seem to mean 'eccentric, freakish, disordered', as for instance in a description of an outré artistic style (in the works of an excellent but admittedly careless English novelist) and applied to a dipsomaniacal writer in an outstanding American film of the 1940s. The overlap between the two senses is small.

R

Received pronunciation

(The American expression is Received Standard.) The Received Pronunciation, often labelled simply RP, is or was not so distant from the so-called Oxford accent or public-school accent or, rather anachronistically, BBC English. The term *accent* is probably more accurate than *pronunciation* for a way of speaking in general.

In the last few years, the expression has become too broad to be very useful. The *COD* (7th edn., 1982) mentions 'local variations', when surely one great thing about the old RP was that it was exactly the same at Land's End as at John o' Groats, not to mention Singapore, and famous for being widely intelligible. It was well defined by a grammarian in 1990 as 'a social accent associated with the upper end of the social-class continuum'. Young speakers of it are becoming rarer than they once were.

Recipe, receipt

The use of *receipt* where most people would use *recipe* continues to this day and is indefensible. It introduces a profit-less ambiguity into a stable situation in which, as everybody knows, *recipe* stands for the formula for producing a particular dish or drink and *receipt* for an acknowledgement of a remittance etc. *Receipt* for *recipe* would count as an example of didacticism if anything of conceivable benefit or interest were being imparted. To use it today is the merest affectation, and if any user mutters it was good enough for her grandmother, ask her if she feels the same about the dentistry her grandmother got, if any, and tell her that such an attitude, if generally adopted, would be a receipt for disaster.

Recourse

This apparently indispensable word is often muddled up with *resort* and *resource*, which both seem to be rather better known. The three all have senses that overlap.

Now: *recourse* means 'a likely means of help', and to *have recourse to* means to 'make use of something (or somebody) as help', so you have recourse to violence or bribery (or good old Jack) to get you out of trouble. In the relevant senses *resort to* means much the same thing, with the attractive availability of the set phrase *last resort*, *last recourse* not being a phrase at all. A *resource* is something valuable you already have in your possession and the word is often used in the plural, so your resources include a large bank-balance and those of America include a stock of natural helium. *Resource* also means 'contrivance, stratagem, device', here approaching an overlap with *recourse*.

That is about the best I can do. My advice is to keep *resort*, especially *last resort*, keep *resources* in plural use, and think about ditching *recourse* altogether. If you find yourself using any of the three, read the whole paragraph through carefully before you publish it. But then you ought to be doing that already, as a matter of routine.

Relevant

This is an example of a former vogue-word that has now become a battered ornament. In a sense, one mourns the passing of a vogue-word as that of a wanker-indicator, but *relevant* was harmful too. Relevant subjects or settings or attitudes or theories are not more blessed than the irrelevant sort, and in some fields irrelevance or apparent irrelevance can be a virtue. There is not much to be said for the kind of person who recommends a children's tale or book for its supposed relevance to the child's experience.

What has moved into the former *relevant* sector is more vogue-words like *insightful*, *innovative* and *ground-breaking*, as in a ground-breaking approach. The third of these is perhaps better considered as a piece of jargon of the hard-to-fathom denomination. Indeed, one or another kind of fortunate coincidence would have been needed to let the outsider know that what is meant is not a ground-breaking approach, whatever that might be, but an approach to a subject or author that supposedly breaks new ground. No doubt it was felt that a new-ground-breaking approach was too advanced an expression for ordinary prose. But the occurrence of any two of this depressing trio (*insightful*, *innovative*, *ground-breaking*) in an article or review is enough to mark its author as a trend-hound of the most committed sort.

Renaissance

I used to be a great one for using the sturdily English form of this word, *renascence*, before I realised how pissily eccentric and difficult it sounded in conversation. Whatever you may write, you are much more likely to be understood if you say *renaissance*, the last syllable rhyming with *ponts* or *ponce*. In the same sort of way I used to try to say *restaurant* like an English word with no final vowel to speak of. Not any more. *Restaront* or *restront* is the spoken English name of the thing.

Residual pronunciations

This catalogue mostly includes pronunciations that seemed
to me not worth an individual note, though it also contains
some remarks on allied topics. It does not set out to be
complete in any way; in particular, it excludes most personal
and place names, and anyone in search of guidance here is
referred to the BBC's pronunciation guides.

abhor. AbHOR with the H sounded.
acoustic. A-COOstic. (Not aCOWstic.)
alas. A-LAHSS. (Not aLASS).
always. AWLwaize is a spelling-pronunciation and AWL-
whizz is the thing to say if you can manage it. I never
really can, having spent most of my life saying ALLwaize
instead. My difficulty is not in remembering to say AWL-
whizz so much as feeling like a fool or Lord David Cecil
when I say it.
analogous. With the G hard as in *get.*
Andrea, Andreas, Anthea. I stress all these names on the
second syllable, having noticed that those who stress the
first one are usually berks.
azure. I try to avoid this word completely, at any rate in
talk, where EHzhur is undoubtedly the thing to say except
that nobody will understand me if I say it.
banal. BuhNAHL. But best avoided completely.
bastard. BAHst'd as term of abuse, of course. The pronunciation BASSt'd is correct for somebody born out of wedlock
but the word is too funny for ordinary talk.
beautiful. To pronounce the middle syllable with a full short
I is pedantic and also non-U. BYOOtuhful is recommended.
berserk. Best avoided completely. Nobody can give the right
pronunciation (stress on first syllable) with a straight face.
Bourbon, bourbon. Meaning a member of that dynastic family
pron. BOORbon. Meaning a kind of chocolate biscuit,

BAWb'n. Meaning a kind of whiskey made from (Indian) corn or maize, BURb'n (from Bourbon County in Kentucky, where first made).

Byzantine. There is a wide choice here. I would use, if I had to use something, bighZANtighn.

cadre. When I was a cadet in the City of London School OTC in the 1930s, this word, meaning the permanent establishment of a training unit like that of one of the Guards regiments, was pronounced CAYder, but no doubt this has lapsed.

Caernarvon. CuhNARv'n.

casual. Only a wanker makes three syllables of this word.

Cecil. As most non-U speakers will show they know, this name is pronounced as if spelt Sissle. Indeed an American of that very name ran a successful jazz band in the 1930s and called it Noble Sissle's Swingsters (featuring Sidney Bechet).

Clwyd. Rhymes with *druid*.

controversy. A well-known trap. Stress on first syllable only, without a secondary stress on the third. Only a berk stresses the second.

cucumber. The name of this plant and its fruit was sometimes pronounced as *cowcumber* by Victorian wits, it seems. More recently, *cowcumber* was a name for a type of wild rhododendron in the southern states of the USA, though by now probably an archaism as well as a rusticism.

Cwmbran. CoomBRAN. First syllable like *cook*, not *doom*.

data. DEHta, not DAHta.

De'Ath. There was a boy at my school so surnamed. He pronounced the name Dih-ATH with a short A. He also had a great many brothers.

dilemma. Pronounce dighLEMMa to remind yourself and perhaps others that the word means, not just a difficulty, but a choice between *two* unpleasant alternatives.

Doreen. I have known only one person who used this forename. She called it D'REEN and was nice enough, but my pronunciation-vote would go to DAWreen. Cf. *Maureen*. *Dyfed*. DUVV-id.

either. I say EYEthuh and you perhaps say EEthuh. Personally speaking, I find the latter a trifle underbred.

envelope. Fully an English word, so pronounce the first syllable EN.

fellow. In ordinary conversation, when 'chap' is meant pronounce FELLa. In any other meaning, especially an academic one, FELLoh.

formidable. Another well-known trap. Only a berk stresses the second syllable. I am not sure what name to attach to the Irish lady who said of some elder French lady that she was rather *formidable*, giving the word something like its French pronunciation as if under the impression that French *formidable* meant formidable.

Genoa. For the Italian city, stress first syllable. For the type of cake presumably first made there, rich, with almonds on top, stress second. Cf. *Seville*.

government. In ordinary talk, two syllables only, GUVm'nt.

graph. Pronounce to rhyme with *gaff*.

Gwynedd. GWINNedh, GWINNuhth, etc.

handkerchief. Best to say HANGkuhchiff, plural HANG-kuhchiffs.

Hertford. Town and college are pronounced HAHf'd. But HARTf'dshuh.

interesting. A word to be careful of. Avoid such remarks in conversation as 'That's interesting,' which implies clearly that what has gone before was and is uninteresting. This may well be true but tactless to convey aloud. Anyway, make it a trisyllable, INtruh-sting. A quadrisyllabic spelling-pronunciation is offensive.

invalid. To mean 'sick person', pronounce INvuhlid. Avoid INvuhleed when I am in earshot.

issue. The pronunciation of this word is perhaps the only point on which I agree with Tony Benn. It is ISHoo, and to say ISSyoo is a piece of pressi-OSSity. So with *tissue*.

Kabul, the capital of Afghanistan. Properly pronounced to rhyme with *bauble*, although when I have to refer to the place, which is seldom, I find I prefer to call it the capital (of Afghanistan).

Keynes. It is Maynard KAYNZ the economist and Milton KEENZ the place.

Llanelly or *Llanelli*, Dyfed. If you must, unlike most of the Welsh, attempt a Welsh pronunciation, at least pronounce the first LL as English L. LuhNETHlih will do very well.

Majorca. The English name, pronounced as an English word. Avoid would-be Spanish – or Mallorquin – noises like Migh-ORca.

Marie. Pronunciation chaotic. Best ask the name-bearer how she pronounces it. Old-fashioned English *Marie* was MAHrih.

Maureen. Proceed as with *Doreen.*

Menzies. Pronounce like an English name unless the bearer is a white-haired Scot, in which case he will tell you.

miniature. Three syllables, MINNy-chuh.

necessarily. Stress on first or third syllable, but avoid nessaSAIRilly.

Newfoundland. The old pronunciation with stressed first syllable is becoming archaic and incomprehensible, so if in doubt stress the second.

ominous. Undoubtedly descended from *omen*, and English *omen* is undoubtedly pronounced OHmen, but for all that *ominous* is pronounced OMMinus, whatever Latinists may say.

pariah. PuhRIGHa.

parliament. Three syllables only: PARlam'nt.

pejorative. Stress on first syllable, like PEE.

peremptory. Stress on first syllable.

poetry. PWETry and POYtry are devilish noises. Make three syllables of it.

Powys. POH-iss.

privacy. PRIVVacy with short I, or PRIGHvacy with long?

Either is correct. My own vote is for the second as more intelligible in talk.

Puerto Rico. The first element is pronounced PORToh.

quasi. Many possibilities. I go for KWEHsigh as more intelligible than some.

Ralph. I realise that in a way I should say Rafe to rhyme with *safe*, but find I can only happily say Ralf. Like most people.

respite. I pronounce this RESSpit with a short I in the second syllable, unlike the long vowel of *COD* and other dictionaries. It is clearly unRESSpittid in Belial's famous *Paradise Lost* speech.

reveille. Stress second syllable and rhyme with *pally*. REVValy nearly rhyming with *Beverley* in US.

romance. RuhMANTS, not ROHmantss.

Sarah. Traditionally SAIRa. But sometimes called SAHra now, as *Clara* is sometimes CLAHra. Some bearers of these names are not clear whether their name is Hebrew or Italian or English. Try asking them how they say it themselves.

scallop, scollop. Always write *scallop* and pronounce SKOLLop.

Seville. For the Spanish city, stress second syllable. For the type of bitter orange and the marmalade made with it, stress first. Cf. *Genoa.*

Smyth, Smythe. If in doubt, say *Smith.* They are mere variant spellings.

Southey. Robert Southey the Lake poet is pronounced SOWDHy, not SUDHy.

status quo. First element STAYtus.

stern. Vocalise the term for the back of a ship like the adjective meaning 'grim'. The pronunciation *starn* is not listed in *COD* and is now archaic. It was never more than a dialectal variant.

Swansea. SWONzy. Nothing to do with swans or sea.

temporarily. Make three syllables of it: TEMPraly.

Theobalds Road. Once TIBBalds. Now as spelt.

tissue. TISHoo, not TISSyou. Cf. *issue.*

tryst. Archaic word, pronounced TRISST or TRIGHSST.

turquoise. Treat as an English word and pronounce TURKwoyze.

(Madam) Tussaud's. (Madam) TOOSSohs. TuhSAWDS is admirable but old-fashioned.

victuals, victualler. VITT'ls, VITler to rhyme with Hitler.

Westminster. WESSminster.

Wodehouse as in P.G. As Woodhouse, not Woadhouse.

zebra. COD gives ZEBBra and ZEEbra. I pick the first. Personally speaking, I find the other a trifle underbred.

Respectively

This serviceable word is sometimes used unnecessarily. When we read that 'the editors respectively of the magazines *Flick* and *Flock* have announced' something, *respectively* tells us that both editors do not edit both magazines, and this might be helpful. But when we read that 'the presidents respectively of Puerto Povre and San Jaime have declared' something, *respectively* tells us only that the two places have a president each and do not share a duumvirate, which most of us could have worked out for ourselves. The lure of *respectively* lies in the impression of careful solemnity it gives, its posh, classical air and its four syllables. The writer of a sentence with *respectively* in it should always check to make sure the word is needed.

Restaurateur

Meaning the proprietor of a restaurant, and so spelt, not as *restauranteur*, I say in the entry on French expressions. The sign *restaurant* on a building or room means that restoring, or restoration, of what Wodehouse calls the vital tissues, by means of food and drink, is available there. Similarly, *café* originally meant that coffee was to be had there, *un dancing* was a hall that offered a band and a dance-floor, and *un camping* is a site where camping is encouraged.

Restauranteur is impossible in French and a pretentious illiteracy in English. But the entry in the latest Roget's *Thesaurus* has the intrusive N and anecdotal and aural evidence suggests that, as often, the illiteracy will shortly replace and render obsolete the true form, in English at least.

Rhythm

This is not the easiest of subjects. The seeker after advice on what rhythm in prose actually is, and how to achieve a kind of prose displaying it to advantage, is not likely to find an answer quickly. One is sometimes tempted to think that anybody with leisure to worry about how a message sounds is not overmasteringly concerned about the content of that message. Nevertheless one or two rules of thumb do emerge.

No careful writer of fiction, that is to say of realistic fiction, will be satisfied with a line of dialogue unless it sounds satisfactory when read out, spoken aloud. It may be less obvious that the writer of any and every kind of prose should also read aloud what it is proposed to print. Nobody who has not habitually done so can imagine the farrago of ineptitudes revealed by this obvious method: unintended rhymes, assonances and repetitions, continual failure of whatever organ might guard against bad sound. If a paragraph of prose is to sound satisfactory to the reader's inner or outer ear, it must already have satisfied its writer by the same criteria.

For all that, when a passage of prose is commended for its rhythmic or sonic beauty, it is often some passage of scripture or high drama or other solemn and emotional writing. This is a little hard on the non-scriptural writer. A meditation on first and last things, not to speak of an account of a human death, is bound to strike the reader as more impressive than a report on the strength of materials. Nevertheless both have their place. It strikes the reader as trenchant and witty when George Orwell rewords a well-known and splendid verse from Ecclesiastes in the style of a government pamphlet, but neither he nor anyone else I know of has tried the same sort of thing the other way round. Specialised expressions, technical terms and such often have the merits of clarity and definiteness, not to mention irreplaceability (if you get what I mean). So no, a *juvenile delinquent* is just that, neither more nor less, and cannot be paraphrased into anything else. And no, it will not do to reword *There is a total lack of ablution facilities* as *There is nowhere to wash*, however funny and brilliant it may be to do so, because those facilities include means of not only washing in general but also of showering, having a bath, shaving, cleaning teeth and washing various bits and pieces and no doubt of other things, all summed up under the admittedly fussy and cacophonous but necessary and concise phrase, *ablution facilities*.

With that said, of course there are plenty of jargon-merchants, those who prefer sonorous, polysyllabic abstractions to plain words, and an eye must be kept out for such, not least within oneself. But to write graceful or stately prose you need a suitable subject with plenty of heavy monosyllables in it, one nearer the Last Judgement than the provision of visual aids and kindred apparatus in pre-teenage educational environments.

Role model

Like TRACK RECORD, this phrase has come into being because of pressure on the bare noun. *Role model* is for those who think that if they say or write *Joyce is a perilous model for young intellectuals* some of the audience may think Joyce is a fashion model or perhaps an artist's model apt to do some unspecified damage to her young intellectual admirers. And if anyone says or writes *Wellington is an excellent model for those intending a military career*, some of the audience may think Wellington reduced to a plastic manikin two inches high would be especially useful to anyone purposefully playing with toy soldiers. And rather than face such eventualities the invention and parrot-like use of a hilarious barbarism like *role model* is surely justified.

S

Sacrilegious

This word earns its place here merely because of the frequency with which it is still, after all this time, wrongly pronounced and spelt as if it had something literal to do with *religious*.

Salutations and valedictions

Occasions when an ordinary person has to write to the Queen or the Archbishop of Canterbury are few and rare, so much so that my observations on how to start such letters are likewise sparse. My advice in such matters is in serious cases to telephone and inquire of one of the secretary-figures by whom those of any grandeur are attended, or should this prove an unattractive option and the need be dire consult a reliable reference-book like *Titles and Forms of Address*, published by A. & C. Black, p. 115 and following.

In practice, the most common kind of formal letter you write is one to the editor of some newspaper or journal or other, and the preliminaries are straightforward enough: To the Editor of the *Budleigh Salterton Guardian* top left and salute that eminence as Sir or Dear Sir, and the newspaper will do the rest. When it comes to signing off, you have the choice of Yours faithfully and Yours sincerely.

Theoretically either of these will do, but your choice in an individual case, like much else, is bound to be influenced by your upbringing and its date. My own were such that I am reluctant to sign myself yours sincerely to anybody I have not actually met. I still remember and feel something of the mild shock I felt when the President of St John's College, Oxford, decent and honest man as I knew him to be, wound up a circular letter to me as one of all of the college undergraduates with this formula in 1945 or possibly early 1946, quite a novelty then. I remember thinking he had every right to call himself mine sincerely at the end of any personal message to me, but slightly less so when he was addressing one and all. Even today I feel a tiny twinge when a correspondent in *The Times* newspaper, unlikely on the face of it to be on amicable terms with the editor, even less the correspondence editor of the publication, closes his letter in those words.

The valediction *Yours, etc.* comes in handy when you want to brush off some intrusive fellow. It is not suitable at any other time.

American usage drops the Yours and merely says Faithfully or Truly or Sincerely. Perhaps originally (and pissily) they wanted to show how egalitarian they were, like calling the children's game follow-*the*-leader. British subjects will avoid.

Same

This little word used to give trouble in a sort of downmarket area, as a mode of saying *ditto* in what were then apt to be called business communications: 'We duly despatched your esteemed order of 2 doz. shirts on 20th inst, and beg to request acknowledgement of receipt of same.' Now *same* has started to upset things in a new sector, in sequence of phraseology. Strictly, *the same* must always be followed by *as* if it is followed at all, so you can say *he wore the same college tie as I did* but not *he wore the same college tie I did* unless you can face being mistaken for an American. Of course you are always free to write *he wore a college tie and I wore the same.* If awkwardness looms, recast the sentence.

Sanction

This mysterious word seems to behave as if at one moment it meant to forbid something and at the next to permit something. The best course is not to set out on any project of reconciliation but simply to take note of the following:

1. *Sanctions* (noun) are a form of economic/military action which, by denying a state or nation the power to import certain materials, seeks to coerce it into certain courses of policy.
2. *Sanction* (noun) is a consideration that operates to enforce obedience to some supposed ethical rule. A sense best avoided in one's own writing.
3. *Sanction* (verb). To sanction a course of action is to declare it justified by the most solemn standards, to ratify or approve it.

A unifying account of the various usages of this word must be possible, but I have never seen a coherent one.

Saxon words

There was a minor craze for these early in this century, giving us all manner of quaint pseudo-archaisms like *skysill* for *horizon*, but it has passed, and with it any notion of a special virtue inherent in 'native' roots. It remains broadly true that, as compared with derivatives of Latin, a decent proportion of Saxonisms in the vocabulary is a sign of a

197

good writer, but the reader should never be allowed to suspect that this is the result of any conscious policy of choice on the writer's part. What 'a decent proportion' amounts to cannot be defined, and it seems easier and safer to approach the problem from the other end and work on the principle that a preponderance of classically derived words in what one writes, especially words denoting abstract qualities or things, especially polysyllables, especially those ending in *-tion* or *-sion*, is a bad sign. That is Rule 1.

Rule 2 annoyingly goes back a little way and says, Never choose to write one word rather than another on the sole ground that it has an Old or Middle English pedigree and its competitor comes from a Latin, French, anyway non-English root. In particular, never choose an English-descended word like *forebear* when a foreign one like *ancestor* seems more familiar and natural.

Rule 3 simply says, as always, read through what you have written and change anything you are not reasonably well satisfied with.

Scotch, Scottish

Best known and most often used world-wide in the form *Scotch*, a noun, the name of a drink. There is much to be said about this, but I will confine myself here to remarking that whereas the legal definition of *whisky* is long and complicated, that of *Scotch whisky* is short and simple, viz. 'whisky made in Scotland'.

Scotch was at one time the preferred form of the adjective in England. Now this has almost disappeared, driven out by *Scottish*, the preferred form north of the Border for over a century, while *Scotsman* has driven out *Scotchman*. The form *Scotch* survives, however, in compounds and set phrases. Nobody talks about *butterscottish* or *hopscots*, and I have never come across a *Scottish egg* or *woodcock*, nor a dendrologist who talked about a *Scottish pine* (by rights he should say a *Scotch fir*, a fir being a kind of evergreen conifer with needles placed singly on the shoots, whereas a true pine has its needles placed in groups of two or more).

The spelling *whisky*, without any E, is preferred for the product of Scotland. *Whiskey*, with the E, is generally used for varieties made in Ireland and the USA.

Secret

At a time when there are apparently no secrets, only revelations of what used to be secrets and perhaps should have remained so, the media apply the adjective *secret* to all sorts of things that have never deserved the label. Thus there may be meetings to discuss a City merger that were nothing more than unreported, but get called *secret*, talks about possible military actions nobody would have honestly called anything but confidential get called *secret*, discussions between two persons of opposite sexes, or even the same sex, are no longer private but *secret*. Oh well, *secret* is a shorter word than some of its possible alternatives, and also tastier and more inviting to the prying and the prurient, and therefore made for headlines – who wants to read about the confirmation of rumours? This is after all no more than a very small victory for trivialisation.

Seek

Except in phrases like *hide-and-seek*, the verb *seek* is little heard in ordinary conversation. Nobody ever asks another if he is seeking trouble or to be funny; the obvious phrases, *looking for* or *trying*, are preferred in informal circumstances. Where *seek* belongs is in formal statements in the media. A management or trade-union spokesman cannot afford to *try* and perhaps fail or *look for* an agreement he may never find. But *seek* and ye shall find, as we were told on a sufficiently solemn occasion, and an agreement both sides are *seeking* sounds almost in the bag. *Seek* in this sense is a politician's word, like *hopefully*.

Semantics

This word (from the Greek *semaino*, I signal or signify or mean) stands for the branch of the study of words which is concerned with their meanings. You might have thought that anything that could possibly help us not to talk nonsense was to be welcomed. There are plenty of people around, however, who dislike having to define their terms, say, when advancing a disputed case, and those who have come across the word in question are likely to say in defence or offence, 'I'm not interested in semantics' in an attempt to reduce their interrogators to the status of mere hair-splitters or nit-pickers. As Johnson said, 'There is no arguing with unresisting imbecility.' One's only dignified recourse is to quit the scene at once, perhaps muttering not very audibly, 'Nor in other things besides,' or some shorter expression.

Sentence

Few readers of these lines will need to be told what a sentence is, but these few include a number who fondly think they know already. Language specialists and others have been busy for decades saying that the old rules are dead, that a sentence is more or less any chunk of wordage anybody cares to sling together, that it is nothing more than a 'part of writing or speech between two full stops or equivalent pauses' (*COD*, 7th edn.). The word *sentence* itself only has definite meaning as a technical term preceded by simple, compound, complex, etc., categories which include subject and predicate, etc.

A sentence, however, is a stylistic as well as a grammatical unit. A written sentence that is technically irreproachable may offend in other ways. One such example is the verbless sentence, acceptable to lexicographers, not necessarily so to ordinary readers, who have stylistic views and expectations whether they know it or not.

The short kind (*Night. April in Paris. What rough beast?*), sometimes in a paragraph of its own, will be readily dismissed as a piece of failed modernism, a vulgarity, a passé shock-tactic. The longer version will almost certainly take longer to identify, moving the reader's eye and attention through several lines of print before letting it be seen that there is no main verb within it, and again plenty of people know what a main verb is who could not set about a definition. They know that an *although* clause, for instance, ought to be subordinate and followed by a *yet all the same* main clause, and feel dissatisfied if none follows. In such cases they have been made to pause without profit, and no self-respecting writer should make a reader do that. A decent line of prose, like a decent line of verse, cannot be expected to yield up its full contents at a single reading, but it must yield up enough to make it plain that to continue at once is a worthy enterprise.

Even today, most of the sentences we come across, including many we hear and never see, contain a main verb and probably other features of the sentences we have met in print, and a great deal would have to change before that is changed and, with it, our expectation of the utterances we encounter.

Sequence of tenses

There is present sequence of tenses and past sequence thereof. Present sequence needs, if anything at all, no more illustration: 'Every day I tell her (that) I love her.' Past sequence may bring problems, consequent on the rule that when a main verb in a sentence is in the past tense, verbs in dependent clauses go to the past tense in sympathy, even though there may be no question of past time elsewhere in such a clause. So when Smith says, 'Every day last week I told her (that) I loved her,' he means 'Every day last week I said to her "I love you",' with no implication that at the end of last week he stopped loving her. But perhaps he feels he must specifically exclude that implication, in which case he would probably say 'Every day last week I told her (that) I love her,' keeping the dependent verb in the present tense to emphasise its present meaning. My own feeling is that, with a topic of such importance, Smith was right to be quite unambiguous, even at the cost of breaking the correct sequence of tenses. That other rule, saying that meanings must be absolutely clear, takes precedence.

Sexist language

The language referred to is English, which regularly includes some less than respectful affix meaning *man* or *masculine* in its words for *female*. The word *female* itself, from *femella*, diminutive of Latin *femina*, assimilates its second syllable to *male*, thus implying that a female is a mere appendage or subsection of a *male*. The ordinary French word for *woman*, known to many readers to be *femme*, eschews both affix and implication.

The English word *woman* carries the process a stage further. The *OED* calls this word 'a formation peculiar to English, and not extant in the earliest period of Old English, the ancient word being *wife* [and its variants].' Thus again, in the word *wife*, a word originally signifying nothing but biological sex becomes one denoting a social relationship in which the man is possessed of and gives his name to the woman. The word *wife* in the sense of old and rustic or uneducated woman, married or not, is still current, especially in dialect and in combinations like *old wife, midwife* and, sometimes fancifully, *fishwife*.

The almost archaic term *lady* is free from any linguistically built-in put-down or sneer, though perhaps none was felt to be necessary in a word originally signifying nothing more than *loaf-kneader* (*hlafdige*) beside a *lord* who at any rate was guard or warden of that loaf (*hlafweard*). Derivations as given in *COD*, etc.

Girl is said, in *COD*, etc., to be perhaps cognate with a Low German word for 'child', nothing more.

The word *she* is actually the modern version of the Old English feminine demonstrative pronoun and adjective, meaning roughly 'that (feminine) one over there'. *He*, in contrast, has always been a regular personal pronoun.

For centuries English writers, in the course of trying to make a point or raise a laugh, have been going on about *woman* and *woe-man*, and Chaucer six hundred or more years ago was being no more than neater than some of his contemporaries when he made a male character say to a female:

> *Mulier est hominis confusio*;
> Madam, the sentence of this Latin is
> Woman is mannes joy and all his bliss.

Chaucer, though well enough educated by the standards of his time, was just possibly unaware that, while *mulier* will do fine to mean woman-as-opposed-to-man, *homo* and its oblique cases will not do as well for man-as-opposed-to-woman and usually means man-as-opposed-to-animal etc. On the other hand it would have been very like Chaucer to pretend to mean the one thing (women throw men into disorder) and all the time mean the other (women throw the human race into disorder). If needed, he had the get-out that he *really* meant the word in its colloquial sense and the *actual* meaning of this Latin is that women throw a fellow into confusion. (Full marks to him for the unobtrusive way he implies that of course no woman understood a word of Latin.)

As far as I know, no English dictionary that gives etymological origins has yet been edited by a female, woman, lady, girl or one of those over there, though such persons can be trusted with revision and kindred tasks.

Shakespeare

It is fair, though hardly very important, that to say or imply that the man of this name is not our greatest writer marks a second-rate person at best. The aberration whereby the name was spelt *Shakspere* is now happily discontinued. I recommend that the derived adjective be spelt *Shakespearean* with an E, not Shake*spearian* with an I.

His works should not be taken as justifying subsequent practice. In particular, as a writer and speaker of the period 1590–1610 he threw accentuation further forward than we now customarily do, making actors in *Hamlet*, for instance, stress *commendable* and *observance* on their first syllables.

Shall and will

In my youth and later, the question of when it was correct to write and say *shall* and *will* (and *should* and *would*) was a matter of continual discussion. Wilson Follett, as unstuffy a man as ever put pen to paper, had twenty-three pages on the question in 1966, and not all the other participants were schoolteachers or swots or petty usage-fanatics or linguists.

Now, however, it has become safe to say that it is nothing but a lonely and diminishing remnant who are even aware that there once was a choice and faintly still is. For good or ill, what H.L. Mencken wrote in 1949, that 'except in the most painstaking and artificial varieties' of the American language the distinction had ceased to exist, has spread out over the English-speaking world.

These days there is no point in rehearsing, for a select few, the various Old-English proto-auxiliary verbs from which our present pair are descended. I offer instead a few scattered remarks which may be of interest and here and there of use. (The rules for *I* also apply to *we* and those for *he* and *she* also apply to *they*.)

At one time there was quite a hard-and-fast rule that said *I shall* denoted simple futurity or prophecy, as in *By this time tomorrow I shall be in Oxford. I will* denoted intention or threat, as in *If you say that again I will (I'll) knock your block off*. By one of those quirks dear to grammarians, this arrangement was reversed with *you* and *he/she/it*, so that *you/he etc. will be there tomorrow* is a mere statement of futurity and *you/he etc. shall* denotes something more, as in *he shall do as he's told*, a rare construction nowadays. If this picture was ever clear it has been fogged by the increased use of contractions such as *I'll, you'll* for *I will/shall* and *you will/shall*.

By a further such quirk, old-fashioned speakers of Scottish-English took that whole arrangement through another 180 degrees. Everybody knows that 'Rule, Britannia' declares at one point, 'Britons never shall be slaves.' What the author, James Thomson, actually wrote was 'Britons never will be slaves,' but he was a Scot. A battered old joke illustrated the difference, as follows. A swimmer in difficulties was heard to shout, 'I will drown and nobody shall save me.' At an inquest on the unfortunate fellow, English jurors wanted a verdict of suicide, Scottish jurors a verdict of death by misadventure, and MacTavish pressed for a rider or footnote rebuking witnesses for making no effort to rescue the victim. Nobody tells that one today.

The words of a song of the Second World War illustrate, no doubt unintentionally, the supposedly traditional role of *will* and *shall*.

There'll be bluebirds over the white cliffs of Dover, sang Dame Vera Lynn, as she later was, *Tomorrow, just you wait and see*, conveying the meaning that the bluebirds would be there one day whether or not anybody did anything about it. There could not be a clearer case of third-person *will* making a mere statement of futurity.

Later in the same song Dame Vera sang:

> *The shepherd shall feed his sheep,*
> *The valley shall bloom again,*
> *And Johnny shall go to sleep*
> *In his own little room again.*

It's tempting here to get distracted by the way the American lyric-writer has exactly caught British rural sentimentality about shepherds and valleys, and also the accuracy of the *Johnny* stuff down to his very name and the form of it. But we must notice the use of *shall* there, indicating not mere futurity but something more, something paraphrasable as, 'I intend to see to it that,' etc. Marcellus, the character in *Hamlet*, put some of the same force into *shall* when trying to warn his prince against wandering into metaphysical danger with the words, *You shall not go, my lord*; it was not Marcellus's fault that Hamlet went regardless. Douglas MacArthur showed a similar grim determination when he promised the Japanese who had thrown him out of the Philippines, *I shall return* (and kept his word).

End of half-digression. What are we to do, faced with a choice of *will* and *shall*, as we still in a sense are even though only a small part of our audience is going to care or even notice, and of that part at least half are sure to be incited by malignant pedantry? The only advice on speech I can give that is likely to be taken is, Bash on regardless, or Do as you've always done. But never say anything that strikes you as unnatural; remember, if it strikes you that way it will certainly strike parts of your audience that way too.

When we move from speaking to writing, many people feel and behave differently. They would rather, or nearly rather, or feel they would rather be stiffly correct than chummily illiterate, especially when writing on their best behaviour, as in a memorial notice. To such people I feel I can offer the following advice:

1. See that you understand the 'hard-and-fast rule' as set out earlier.
2. Decide how important it is to you to follow this rule rather than the dictates of what, on consideration, seems to you natural and unaffected.
3. Proceed accordingly, remembering the two golden rules that really are rules: don't write anything that seems to you barbarous, and you can always recast the sentence.
4. But not before having read me on SHOULD AND WOULD.

She and it

Until quite recent times any country was apt to be personified in certain contexts, almost always in the form of a woman, as in our own cases. The United Kingdom, then often called England, was mother of the free, and *motherland*, although nowadays it has an archaic ring, stayed in the dictionary as meaning one's native country. Nowadays, again, the usual and operative pronoun is not *she* but *it*, so firmly so that to speak or write of one's country as *she* invites genuine incomprehension or else a faint hostility as 'jingoistic'.

There are countries, Castro's Cuba for example, that one would hesitate to speak of as any kind of person, indeed even to call them *it* may seem a little on the flowery side. But there are others, like our own, still decent enough to be personified, and to make it harder, even by a small amount, to feel a personal attachment to the place and its ways is surely undesirable, however 'jingoistic' the alternative.

I seem to remember that the Church too was once referred to as *she*, but can find no authoritative confirmation.

Shibboleth

A *shibboleth* is defined in *COD* as a noun meaning 'test word or principle or behaviour or opinion, the use of or inability to use which reveals one's party, nationality, orthodoxy, etc. (see Judg. 12:6); catchword,' and so on. At the end comes the pedigree of the relevant Hebrew noun, *sibbolet* with a couple of diacritical marks, meaning 'ear of corn' though the scholiast differs – but the meaning is irrelevant here. But the OT Book of Judges 12 is relevant enough.

Two armed factions in ancient Palestine, Gileadites and Ephraimites, had quarrelled and the Gileadites under Jephtha had won. A surviving Ephraimite tried here and there to pass himself off as a returned Gileadite, without success as it appears:

> . . . the men of Gilead said unto him, Art thou an Ephraimite? If he said, Nay: Then said they unto him, Say now Shibboleth: and he said Sibboleth: for he could not frame to pronounce it right. Then they took him, and slew him at the passages of Jordan . . .

Failure to pronounce a word right today seldom brings such dire consequences; nevertheless, it is always rewarding to spot a would-be dissembler or infiltrator. Most Welsh people, now, make no bones about being the genuine article, and quite right too, but there are those among them who, like their English neighbours, try to pass themselves off as having come from a posher background than the one they grew up in. The shibboleth-word in such cases is sometimes said to be *situation*. Fearful of putting in a giveaway consonantal-*y*-sound as in *flyoo* or *scryoo*, the aspirant over-corrects by leaving it out this time round and says *sitooation*, unlike most of those east of Offa's Dyke; Lord Jenkins himself tumbles down here. My own Welsh shibboleth is a word like *longer* or *stronger*, which the unwary Welshman will pronounce without the guttural force of the G, unlike, say, *conga*. I had always wondered a little about the poet Sir John Davies (1569–1626) until I caught him rhyming *finger* with *singer*, which secured him for ever in my esteem as a true Taff.

For a shibboleth to persist over centuries is nothing; I think I have identified one that spans millennia. In *Coronation Street* on television, the decent Moroccan character Samir or Sameer now pronounces his name like Sam-EER, instead of Sham-EER as earlier. The reason for the change was given out as that only Israelis pronounce that kind of initial S as SH; others in that part of the world, including Moroccans, kick off with a plain S. So after all this time the heirs of the Ephraimites are *still* saying S where their rivals are *still* saying SH, though without the unpleasant consequences noted in the years BC. At the moment, anyway.

Should and would

Over the last couple of generations, *will* has been pushing out *shall*. Over a similar period, *would* has even more effectively been pushing out *should*. There are several possible reasons for this.

1. *I'd* for *I should* as well as *I would* seems even easier to slip into than *I'll* for *I shall* as well as *I will*.
2. The *should* area is complicated by notions of duty and obligation (e.g. *this is not a matter of what I want to do but of what I should do*) in a way and to a degree that the *shall* area is not.
3. The construction *I should do such-and-such* without the follow-up of *if I were you* or *in your place* has grown to the point where *I should* has increasingly become a verb of advising or recommending rather than one of consequence.
4. Nobody has ever said *I should if I could*.
5. Influence from America has made *I would think so* seem more the expression of a personal opinion and more tentative than *I should think so*.

It seems to me quite likely that *I should*, as any sort of past tense of *I shall*, will in another couple of generations be as archaic as *I ween*.

Simplistic

This is a recent usage – first recorded 1881, but not popular for a century or more – and a handy put-down word. By its use, what you thought was simple – straightforward, obvious, clear – is transfigured in a flash into simple-minded, credulous, naive:

The simplistic view that criminals are born, not made.

Simplistic theories of the genetic transmission of intelligence.

Now it may well be that such views and theories are indeed simple-minded or advanced by the simple-minded, but that is not the issue. The word *simplistic* is perfect for its usual job, that of gracefully dismissing something without discussing it.

The something so dismissed is more often than not on the political Right and the dismisser even more often on the Left. No word suggests itself as an equivalent weapon for the Right, which has to fall back on tattered labels like *old-hat, crackpot, airy-fairy, half-baked*. But then the Right has often been old-hat in the past and the Left good at devising new words and new usages.

Single-handedly

Some illiteracies are presented in the name of literacy, or at least of regularity and common sense. This is a popular one just now. Those who like to make words longer and more polysyllabic have not noticed or do not care that *single-handed* is already an adverb as well as an adjective, and expressions like *he saw it through single-handed* are used and effortlessly accepted a thousand times a day. The lately fashionable *overly*, one of the ugliest intruders of this part of the century, is similarly an unnecessary extension of what was already a thriving and unquestioned adverb.

There are plenty of other adverbs vulnerable to creative illiteracy through not ending in *-ly*. *Regardless* is in the forefront, having three syllables already and perhaps standing in need of rehabilitation by being blown up into *irregardless* by a different kind of illiteracy. But no word of this sort – an adverb not already ending in -*ly* – can be considered safe. When can we expect to see *quitely? Altogetherly? What nextly?*

The foregoing can be seen as a gallant attempt to ridicule what may be cause for more than a passing irritation. An award-winning actress was recently witnessed on television thanking all those who had contributed to her triumph, 'lastly but not leastly' some easily overlooked minor figure. And a New York dentist says 'open widely' on his best behaviour, but 'open big' when in a hurry. Everybody speaks more formally at some times than at others, but putting on airs with what is a solecism as well as an absurdity is to be deplored.

Snootiness

I have given an unpleasant name (it supposedly derives from *snout*) to an unpleasant thing, a name that at any rate has an English root and therefore befits a very English thing. I like and admire the English character as much as anybody does, I think, but this is and for a long time has been a grave weakness in it.

To strike up outside the home key: I have heard it suggested that English snootiness lost the African empire that English enterprise and magnanimity had helped to acquire, lost the hearts and minds of the colonialised nations as well as sovereignty over their territories. French behaviour to indigenous peoples was probably harsher than ours was, but the post-imperial descendants of those peoples, in spheres like poetry and cuisine, seem closer to the French than our former subjects do to us. One important reason is the persistence of English snootiness. A man will perhaps forgive or agree to overlook a kick in the stomach more readily than a snub. Here is another word for a kind of nose, which organ features in several allied expressions. *Toffee-nosed*, more properly *toffy-nosed*, toffish-nosed, *toff* being an earlier coinage than *toffee/taffy*, is one of these, *turn up one's nose* another. The image is of a supposed aristocrat keeping his nose loftily above the level of the malodorous common herd.

To demonstrate that we have not actually left linguistic matters behind, let me suggest to the reader that Chesterton perfectly characterised the English snub in two spoken sentences, one the apparent statement, 'No doubt you're right,' said as to mean, 'No doubt you think you're right,' and the apparent query, 'You think so?' said so as to convey the follow-up, 'You would.' A couple of rounds of this sort of thing, rubbed in with a snooty lifting of the nose and a refusal to shake hands, another English ruling-class habit, and superiority is entrenched beyond removal even by immediate violence.

The African empire and all such things are vanished now, but English snootiness is not. Its survivals are none of my concern here unless as features of style of utterance. I admit I am quite likely seeing what is not there when I find a contemporary version of it in the pervasive unspecific irony with which journalists treat the people and subjects they comment upon in columns and sketches. No doubt every culture has its modes of non-committal superiority of manner, not that anything very heinous is at stake here. But the snub rather than any sort of rude remark is still the distinctive English way of winning the upper ground.

Not so long ago it was fashionable to indicate superiority by insincerely apologising for the use of slang or a cliché with some formula as 'to use the vernacular expression'. Now slang itself is fashionable, but the habit of seeming self-reproach has not disappeared. People still say, even if they seldom write, 'to coin a phrase' or 'if you'll pardon the expression' when letting fall wordage they consider beneath them, though they may assume a self-mocking tone in which to do so, and some of the self-mockery may be genuine.

213

The subtlest and most tenacious method of using low expressions and preserving dignity is to hang inverted commas round them, a habit first noticeable in the works of Henry James. This is an attempt to have it both ways. It would be hard to set out briefly what the courtesy light in a car is and does, and yet the phrase is the manufacturer's, so stick it in quotes and directness is achieved without loss of dignity. Or so the writer hopes. The reader perhaps wants to yell, 'Either have the courage of your clichés and use them without apology or work harder at devising alternatives. More shortly, get off your high horse.'

So far and no further

As was for many years inevitable, derivatives of *far* have been driven out by those of *fore* or *fur*, and it is now correct to say and write *further* and *furthest* in all meanings and contexts. *Farther* and *farthest* are still fully intelligible, at least when written, but avoided in use.

I once heard the word *fur* used as a primary, positive adverb – 'it's not too fur down the road from here' – by a batman-driver in 1944. Unless the speaker was back-forming from *further* or *furthest*, which of course is quite possible though I judge unlikely, this suggests an original form quite distinct from *fore*. In any case, as everybody knows, *far* remains the positive form in use alongside comparative and superlative expansions not directly derived from it.

Some

The recent history of this little word is a good example of the perpetual dynamism of linguistic error, its tireless search for new prey, however insignificant on the face of it. The realms of pronunciation and stress, being less easy to write about than the word on the page, are especially inviting. So it is coming to be with *some*.

A useful distinction had grown up whereby *some* in the sense of 'some but not others' (sense 1, as in 'some problems are easily solved') had come to be pronounced *sum*, with full value given to the vowel, whereas *some* in the sense of 'an unspecified number or amount' (sense 2, as in 'have some sandwiches, have some tea') had come to be pronounced *s'm*. Now, sense 1 is increasingly pronounced as in sense 2 and sense 2 as in sense 1. To be invited to 'have *sum* tea' is intelligible enough and suggests nothing more damaging than that the speaker hails from the North of England, or is a victim of the current quasi-pedantic craze for giving such vowels their full value. But to be told over the radio, say, that '*s'm* recent Cabinet decisions have been very unpopular, while others . . .' may be baffling, not for long but perhaps for long enough to cause the listener to lose the thread of the first part of the sentence. If broadcasters would go to the burdensome length of reading their words before starting to say them, this and similar mild annoyances might be avoided.

Spelling mistakes

These are, perhaps unexpectedly, less common in tabloid newspapers with a high circulation than in the so-called quality Press. This is probably because the tabloids are more heavily sub-edited than the others, no doubt in pursuit of base objectives like uniformity, but uniformity in pursuit of correct spelling is hardly base at all. It is reassuring to find that there are still enough good spellers to go round.

The qualities commit fewer vulgarities and barbarisms of language, not least in their main headlines, but the greater freedom their contributors enjoy extends to eccentricities of spelling. It is in those columns and long articles that you will quite often find the *Meditteranean* and *Carribean* Seas, British *ex-patriots*, some of them *dessicated*, *miniscular* objections and things *loveable* and *forgiveable* (though Friday's child has yet to be *loveing* and *giveing*), not to speak of difficulties with hyphens (though these infest the tabloids too) and, just the other week and twice over in *The Times*, *pantomine* (though perhaps this was not so much a spelling mistake as just a mistake).

Of the many arguments for avoiding incorrect spelling I would choose two. One is that neglect of this precaution goes down badly with people, including some who may be thought generally unworthy but whose disapproval may be worth avoiding. The other argument is more in the nature of an appeal. If writing is worth doing it should be done as well as possible. Waiting at table is also worth doing, and simple pride should prevent a waiter from serving from dirty plates and with dirty hands. And the waiter will have a better time of it too with clean plates and clean hands.

Spelling reform

Some tender-hearted or woolly-headed observers have noticed that English spelling is often inconsistent or worse, and that children and foreigners, not to mention a few adult native speakers not otherwise unintelligent, find difficulty with it. Such observers sometimes go on to urge spelling reform, perhaps being in a position to know that Webster of dictionary fame happened to be a mild reformer (hence American *color*, *center*, *traveler*, etc.) and nobody has complained. So why not go further?

The reasons why not are various, starting with the fact that by accident or design, probably design, Webster went about as far as it was safe to go. The next point is that

English vowel-sounds change from one position to another, so that *fraternise*, for example, gives something like FRATT-uh-nise whereas *fraternity*, very much part of the same language-family, gives fruh-TERR-nity. Next, sounds change from place to place even within these islands, so both the *fraternal* words acquire a detectable R in west-of-England speech not spoken or heard in south-eastern England. And what about Yorkshire, Glasgow, Belfast, not to speak of other places where they speak English from the cradle, like America in all its variety, Australia, New Zealand and a host of places I cannot list here?

Economic even more than linguistic obstacles impede any programme of spelling reform. The cost of republishing all extant literature in any such spelling would be prohibitive. And that of banishing millions of literate people from the existing community of English-readers – for nothing else would be entailed by any selective plan – is not to be reckoned fiscally.

No. It is more realistic, more merciful and finally more blessed to keep on beavering away with *I before E except after C* (if they still teach that) and resigning oneself to the prospect that some people will always be better spellers than others.

Split infinitive

This, the saying or writing of *to really think*, *to boldly go*, etc., is the best known of the imaginary rules that petty linguistic tyrants seek to lay upon the English language. There is no grammatical reason whatever against splitting an infinitive and often the avoidance of one lands the writer in trouble, as in Fowler's example:

The men are declared strongly to favour a strike.

Here, in the course of evading the suspect *to strongly favour*, the writer has left the reader in some doubt whether *strongly* applies to the declaring or the favouring. As Fowler remarks elsewhere in his article:

> It is of no avail merely to fling oneself desperately out of temptation; one must do it so that no traces of the struggle remain; that is, sentences must be thoroughly remodelled instead of having a word lifted from its original place and dumped elsewhere.

A warning that every writer, at least, should take generally to heart. Towards the end of the piece, Fowler lays down his recommended policy:

> We will split infinitives rather than be barbarous or artificial; more than that, we will freely admit that sufficient recasting will get rid of any s[plit] i[nfinitive] without involving either of those faults, [and] yet reserve to ourselves the right of deciding in each case whether recasting is worth while.

The whole Fowler notice deserves and repays perusal, all 1800-odd words of it. See *MEU*, pp. 558–561.

That last sentence of his is as true as any such sentence can be. But although he was writing nearly seventy years ago, the 'rule' against split infinitives shows no signs of yielding to reason. This fact prompts some gloomy conclusions. One such is that anti-split-infinitive fanatics are beyond reason. Another is that, whatever anybody may say, split infinitives are still to be avoided in most circumstances. Consider: people with strong erroneous views about 'correct' English are just the sort of people who consider your application for a job, decide whether you are 'educated' or not, wonder about your general suitability for this and that (e.g. your inclusion in a reading list). Do you want to be right or do you want to get on? – sorry, to succeed. I personally think that to split an infinitive is perfectly legitimate, but I do my best never to split one in public and I would certainly not advise anybody else to do so, even today.

Today we have reached a point at which some of our grammatical martinets have not actually been taught grammar, with the result that they are as hard as ever on the big SI without being at all clear what it is. Indeed, even their slightly better-educated predecessors were often shaky on the point, seeming to think that a phrase like 'X is thought to be easily led' contained an example. Any ungainly departure from natural word-order is likely to betray a fear that a splittable infinitive may be lurking somewhere in the reeds. When a correspondent, a self-declared Yorkshireman, demands of the editor of *The Times*, 'Have you lost completely your sense of proportion?' seasoned campaigners will sniff the air, in this case and others without result. But nobody is ever quite safe.

Splitting words

It was in 1985 that Fleet Street switched over from old-fashioned methods of type-setting to the new technology involving computers, such that you effectively typed your article straight into the columns of the newspaper. One result of this move was that the splitting of words between lines of print, formerly the outcome of entirely human choice, became semi-automated and therefore declined sharply in quality. It was nothing for a word to start at the end of one line as *cha* or *chan* or *chang* and end at the start of the next with *nging* or *ging* or *ing* or *ed*. After some years of gross discourtesy to the reader, who without warning had to juggle mentally with uncouth fragments of words in the hope of arriving at a recognisable whole like *changing* or *changed*, the position improved somewhat. The days of *penk-nives*, *studi-os* and *stren-gth* were over, or at least numbered. Dismaying gaps appear to this day in what would formerly have been close lines of type, and quite often such lines fail to extend to the end of a column, but in general things have become only about half as bad as they were after progress had first struck.

There are (at least) two kinds of affront left to complain about – no more effective step seems open. One is the occurrence of compounds like *pre-historic* and *un-usable* in ordinary lines of print, the doing presumably of someone whose computer has been inadequately briefed. Another comes from a consensus of error whereby *England* and *English* etc. are split *En-glish* etc. instead of *Eng-lish* etc. Now I may be seeing things where nothing is, but we live in what was once called something like *Angle-land*, not in any precursor of *En* or *gland*, so can it not be *Eng-lish* and *Eng-land* from now on?

The 1993 *Collins Gem Dictionary of English Spelling* includes, as it says on its cover, 'complete hyphenation guidance', i.e. to whether and where you may split words. It is mostly quite sound on *change*, though it permits *changing* (to rhyme with *banging*, *clanging*, etc.?), but it does list *Eng-land* and *Eng-lish* and seems in general trustworthy.

Sucking pig

This is the ordinary name for a piglet not yet weaned, whether considered as an animal or as a dish. However, one often hears and sees the similar expression *suckling-pig*, evidently meaning the same thing. I suspect the alternative of being an Americanism, perhaps an ancient one, of the crypto-puritanical sort like *roach* (British *cockroach*) or *rooster* (British *cock*) that infiltrated supposedly more tasteful variants or downright changes of the original. The gain in tastefulness from *sucking* to *suckling* may seem small, but every little helps, as the old lady said when she made water into the sea.

Sycophant

Part of the history of this word illustrates the folly of trying to explain the meaning of a word by its origin. The word *sycophant* derives straightforwardly enough from a Greek word which transliterates as *sukophantes*, which descends no less straightforwardly from two shorter words, *sukon* a fig and *phaino* I show. Then the trouble starts. The longer word is said in the authoritative Liddell and Scott *Greek-English Lexicon* to be:

> properly *a fig-shewer*,* i.e. *one who brings figs to light by shaking the tree*: or *a fig-informer*, i.e. *one who informs against persons exporting figs* from Attica [of which Athens was the principal city], but used in the sense of *a common informer, a false accuser, slanderer*.

Really? How *a fig-shewer* came to mean *a common informer* is not explained, nor how either came to mean what the word means in English, *a flatterer, toady or parasitic person*. The big *OED* rightly washes its hands of the matter: '[not] satisfactorily accounted for . . . cannot be substantiated . . .' The comparatively small *COD* sensibly gave the ruling, at least until 1970, 'reason for name unkn[own]', but then in 1988 amended this to 'reason for name uncer[tain]', so perhaps some new fantasy or guess is in preparation.

Surely any true friend of the language, one who wants to treat it and its predecessors as more than 'a philological playground' in Fowler's own words, will agree that the origin of *sycophant* is undiscoverable, and leave it at that. The importance of historical origins as a guide to meaning has seldom been so convincingly given the lie to.

---

* One who shews or more familiarly shows figs. To write *a fig-shower* might mislead.

Symbolic forms

Anxious readers may need to be reassured that they are not about to be told anything whatever about symbolism in the graphic or literary arts. A symbolic form in a language describes (not perhaps very satisfactorily) that class of word that stands somewhere between onomatopoeic words like *cuckoo* and *sizzle* on the one hand and ordinary non-echoic words like *beauty* and *bedstead* on the other. As one authority puts it, such forms 'have a connotation of somehow illustrating the meaning more immediately than do ordinary speech-forms'. There is no shortage of words that sound rather similar and have a meaning in the same rough area. Famous examples include some that begin with the cluster *gl* and others that end with the sound *ump*. The first group seem to have something to do with steady light, for instance *glow, glare, glimmer, gleam, glint, gloaming*, the second with the idea of clumsiness, like *hump, clump* (he *clumped* along), *chump, lump, stump* and several more. Why or how this sort of thing happens nobody seems to know, but it does happen in other languages without any points of agreement emerging.

One symbolic group that has not attracted so much attention is typified by the word *pig*. 'Rightly is they called pigs,' said some fictional character, presumably a townsman, after a look at life in the sty. So it could be a term of contempt or even loathing, whether applied by an old-fashioned farmer to a domesticated animal or by a slightly less old-fashioned demonstrator to a policeman. That demonstrator might care to know, by the way, that that use of *pig* was first recorded in the year 1812, only a dozen years after the first policemen or such figure appeared in London. Meaning the animal, *pig* began to drive out the older word *swine* in the early nineteenth century, meaning a person probably about 1860.

Pig, it will be readily agreed, is a monosyllable (therefore emphatic) beginning with the sound *pi-*. There are only a limited number of these possible in English, but three of them do, or can, carry contempt: *pimp*, the archaic exclamation *pish*, and good old *piss*, a term of strong execration when uttered on its own. Several words in the *pig* group are indelicate, therefore likely to carry strong feeling. If we pull back to include monosyllables just beginning with the letter P, the list is much longer: *pah, pap, poke, pox, podge, pooh, poop* (archaic childish term for excrement), *pulp, pus, poof, poove, ponce, punk* (which meant a prostitute in the eighteenth century and earlier). The sound *puh* is tailor-made to express contempt, with the puff of breath that goes with it at the beginning of an English word making it almost a word in itself.

To take the other end of the word, of monosyllables with a short vowel ending in *-g*, a large number again convey contempt, some of them again indelicate and several of them slang: *bag, cag, drag, fag, slag, nag* (in two senses), *shag, hag, dreg, prig* (archaic slang for a thief), *frig, bog, hog, wog, quag* (mire), *bug* (in two senses), *slug, mug* (in two senses), *smug* – and when we meet Silas *Wegg* in *Our Mutual Friend*, we know at once he will be up to no good.

Finally, the special, restricted cases, monosyllables beginning with P and ending with G. Not many are possible, and most of them are not words at all; as far as I know there is no *pag*, no *pog*, no *poog* in English. By my count there are only two. *Pug* is not contemptuous when applied to a breed of dog, but *pug-nosed* is offensive, to call a boxer a *pug* is offensive even though the word may derive from *pugilist*, and at various times in the past *pug* has meant an ape, a dwarf and, as before, a prostitute. The only other possibility is *peg*, pretty innocuous on the face of it, but once used as a verb meaning to gorge, to overeat, so perhaps I pick up half a mark there.

All in all, then, if anyone had been commissioned to run up a word to convey emphatic contempt on the brink of downright loathing, that person could not have bettered the one commonly applied to *porcus domesticus* and to human beings regarded as being of the same status. So absolutely rightly is they called pigs.

T

Thankfully

Not an illiteracy in sentences like, 'After my long walk in the sun I thankfully put down a glass of shandy,' where the walker/drinker is thankful. But a stark illiteracy in, say, 'Thankfully, the shandy was well chilled,' where nobody in particular is thankful. A word like *luckily* is required instead.

The use of *thankfully* in a dangling position, however, as in my second example just above, is not a politician's use like that of dangling *hopefully*. It makes no attempt to smuggle in more than it says, even though it is a warmer sort of word than *luckily*. In any case, this is a use that looks likely to catch on further with or without the approval of honest writers, who will go on avoiding it.

That, which, who

This is an old trap, or crux. Any full treatment of it is bound to cover a lot of space: the position about these relative pronouns takes up some 3000 words of *MEU*, words I would not dare to try to summarise. Instead, I offer a few pieces of advice on the question of when it is correct to write 'the book *that* I was reading' and when 'the book *which* I was reading'.

1. Remember, or take note, before you start that plenty of good writers have got this one wrong now and again

and plenty of bad writers have got it right. It will help some aspirants to say they prefer to sin with Shakespeare than to be virtuous with – I leave the choice to them. Those of sterner stuff will prefer to sin as little as possible.

2. The problem is often duckable by omitting any pronoun and writing 'the book I was reading' or its equivalent, as I did after the comma in the second sentence of this article.

3. Sentences of the general type of 'the book I was reading' will do for virtually any kind of speaking and most kinds of writing. In formal prose, however, many people will feel a *which* or a *that*, one or the other, is required of them.

4. Although the word *that* as a relative pronoun is the more common of the two in speech, *which* is in no way the posher or grander or more literary or more 'correct' of the two, and the sub-editor who went through a friend's typescript changing every relative *that* to *which* was wrong as well as intolerably cheeky.

5. When a relative pronoun is required, the rule is that defining clauses are introduced by *that*, and others, non-defining or informative ones, by *which*. If this sounds horrible, just keep repeating *This is the house that Jack built*. Let us distinguish between two possibilities:

   This is the house that Jack built, not the one that anyone else built. The house is defined as the one that *Jack* built.

   This is the house, which Jack built or caused to be built with the money he inherited from his uncle Herbert, who . . . Note the comma after *house*. We are given information about this house and its building, but the house is not defined as the one that Jack built.

6. The picture remains essentially the same when people, not things, are involved, as comparison between the two following specimens will show.

   This is the man that I spoke to, less satisfactorily but to some tastes more respectfully put as *This is the man whom I spoke to*, a construction to be careful of in one's own writings. See 7.

This is the man, whom I spoke to for several minutes and recognised without difficulty as . . . Not, again, the comma after *man*.

7. Confusions may arise when the writer becomes nervous of the length of his defining clause and puts in a pair of commas that make the clause seem like a non-defining one, as in:

Young children, who are undersized and unprepossessing and have none of the qualities other children admire, may need special attention.

Here he has inadvertently committed himself to a statement that *all* young children are undersized, etc. Easily avoided, as for instance by:

Some young children, those who are undersized, etc., may need special attention.

The amount of rewriting necessary in this case is small, but it turns nonsense into sense. This is often the case.

Thesaurus

The only thesaurus mentionable here is the 1000-page lexicon of English synonyms and near-synonyms first published by P.M. Roget in 1852. Roget (1779–1869) was many things, including a practising doctor of medicine, a secretary of the Royal Society and an original member of the Senate of London University. In his preface to the first edition he said he had completed a smaller version for his own use which he started to enlarge and prepare for publication on retirement from his secretaryship.

Unfortunately, Roget was very much a man of his time in his intellectual processes and his general view of such things, and he classified his word-lists into thematic divisions like 1 – Abstract Relations, Section *1*, Existence, *2*, Relation and so on to the extent of dozens of sub-headings. But fortunately these can be totally ignored without noticeable loss. At such a distance Roget's classifications look pretty archaic to me and I have never even tried to make sense of them, nor has anyone else I know of. His thesaurus does not seem to suffer thereby.

A synonym is a word that means the same thing as another. It has been said that there are only two pairs of perfect synonyms in English, *almost* and *nearly* and *commence* and *begin*. On inspection even these show differences. Unlike *nearly*, *almost* can qualify a noun, as in Philip Larkin's reference to 'our almost-instinct'; *nearly*, unlike *almost*, means 'closely' in the first place. *Commence* and *begin* are more synonymous in a way, but only someone with no feeling for words would treat them as interchangeable. What Roget did is group words and phrases in roughly the same area of meaning, as in:

885 DISCOURTESY – N. *discourtesy*, impoliteness, bad manners, disgraceful table m.; no manners, want of courtesy, lack of politeness, lack of manners, incivility, churlishness, uncouthness, boorishness, yobbishness 847 *ill-breeding*; unpleasantness, nastiness, misbehaviour, misconduct, unbecoming conduct; tactlessness, want of consideration, stepping on one's toes.

The *Thesaurus* is far from perfect, but it is essential for those interested in language and also for those writers who merely want to find a suitable word.

Till and until

Fowler says roundly and twice over that *till* is the 'usual' form and chides *until* as 'giving a certain leisurely or deliberate or pompous air' to the context, though he concedes that 'when the clause or phrase precedes the main sentence, *until* is perhaps actually the commoner.' All this remains true, and the only point of this entry is to reassure anyone who needs it that *till* is a genuine English preposition and conjunction with its roots in Old English and Old Norse and is not a daringly informal shortening of stuffy old upperclass *until* and spelt *'til*.

Too

Too is sometimes used by Americans, and increasingly here, to mean *very*, as in *I don't feel too well*. This colloquial use is surely unobjectionable and does not even need an eye kept on it, unlike many a potential abuse. A student, a young American, I had the duty of supervising on a creative writing course (poetry division) once defended himself against the charge of wilful obscurity by pleading to me, 'Sir, I guess I don't pay too much heed to the reader.' Would that other shortcomings of our pupils contained their own demolition so neatly.

Never begin a fresh sentence with *too* followed by a comma, to mean something like *further* or *also*. Not even Americans should be allowed to get away with that.

Track record

These days, no politician or other public figure in good standing has anything else but a *track record*. He or she cannot have just a *record* any more because that is what a convicted criminal has. The phrase is a good example of the kind of thing that is perfectly harmless in newspaper use (however nasty the grin of recognition it may arouse) and not at all harmless in any attempt at anything at all serious. (Another good example is ROLE MODEL. Nobody can just be a *model* any more because the word means somebody who displays garments etc. by wearing them in a photograph.)

Transpire

This famous misuse, which consists in trying to make the word mean simply 'happen' instead of 'leak out, come to be known', is still with us after nearly a century of denunciation. One bar to its destruction has perhaps been the difficulty of deciding whether the word is intended to mean 'happen' or 'come to be known' in familiar contexts like 'such abuses seldom transpire in a democracy'. Another has perhaps been the difficulty of making up one's mind to bother, if that is not just an admission of defeat.

Twice two

Whether you should say twice two *is* four or *are* four was the sort of 'argument' people interested in words were sometimes asked to 'settle'. All right, then: either is correct, and the two have been so for half a dozen centuries. The *was* and *were* in the first sentence are in the past tense because the problem involves some acquaintance with multiplication. Next question.

Two cheers for only connect

It is not necessary to be bored by the novels of E.M. Forster as much as I am in order to be fed up with a couple of slogans he started on their course, one of them contained in a novel of 1910, the other part of a title of 1951. As far too many people will be aware, they are 'only connect' and 'two cheers' for some abstraction or other, 'democracy' in the original.

1. Only connect. It seems hopelessly vague as a guide to conduct, whatever Forster may have meant, and the context is a poor interpreter. Perhaps the maxim calls upon the writer to be on the look-out for similarities in behaviour or character and nothing else. Or does it mean that the mere demonstration that something is connected to something else is enough in itself and that nothing needs explaining or discussing? Or is it just a phrase that comes in handy for those who want to seem profound but have nothing very definite to say?

2. Two cheers were probably as many as Forster could manage in favour of anything, from democracy to stamp-collecting, that is to say anything bodiless. His avowal, that he only had two cheers to spare for the system that he was able to flourish under, has brought him some undeserved respect as well as doing its bit to reinforce political quietism. The Forsters of this world go on as if they would prefer to be spared the vulgarities entailed in running a decent society, one which deserves four cheers from its citizens and others too.

Typewriter vs. word-processor

This book, like all my others, even the most recent, was written not on a word-processor but a typewriter. Currently this is what it has been for the last thirty years, an Adler office model of the acoustic (i.e. non-electrical) sort, a characteristic it shares with all its forerunners. I stick to my alphabet piano in the first place for reasons to do with age, habit, experience, tight-fistedness and so on, but not for those alone.

Some years ago, a leading firm that made word-processors asked me and other worthies of that era (Stirling Moss, Humphrey Lyttelton et al.) to let them have a few words saying how much we liked word-processors, especially those of that particular make. I found it hard to think of ways how and reasons why, but the fee was an actual word-processor, brand new and instantly floggable. Even so I came to feel quite sorry for the nice young fellow from the advertising agency who trudged up to my house in Kentish Town to quiz me on such points.

'I expect you've often found these things pretty useful in your walk of life,' he began.

'I've never used one,' I said.

'Oh. Well, I expect you've often found you can remember the first two or three letters of a word but not the rest, haven't you?'

'No, never, as it happens.'

'Oh. Well, there's a dictionary with 80,000 words in it available in there,' he said, referring to the piece of machinery on the table between us.

'There's a dictionary with 150,000 words in it available there,' I said, giving my *Concise Oxford* a friendly glance.

'Oh. Well, what can I say you said, for Christ's sake?'

What I eventually let him say I said was that the word-processor would change a character's name, as it might be from Herbert to Charlie, in the twinkling of an eye and without any exceptions throughout a piece of writing. I did not make him say I said that I could manage that unassisted, without benefit of word-processor, when I came to re-type. Nor did I make him record our brief chinwag when I asked him whether, using a word-processor, I could go on having access to my first thoughts the way I could with a typewriter.

'Sorry?' he said.

I explained, or reminded him, how after x-ing out one's first thoughts on a typewriter and putting in a corrected version one could still see what one's first thoughts had been and perhaps derive benefit from them.

'Oh yes, I remember doing that,' he said.

'Well, could you do anything like that on a word-processor?'

This time he understood. 'No,' he said.

That was enough to make me decide to stick to my typewriter. But then the word-processor people had the last laugh by giving me only an obsolescent model to flog round the place when I reached the stage of realising my fee.

My feelings about word-processors, already cool, were further lowered when a friend told me how he had blotted out, simply by pressing the wrong button, the whole of a speech he had written to be delivered at his old school. I happen to be less than good at buttons and am anyway not by any manner of means the one to risk losing a whole novel that way, or even a whole line of one. In any case, most words you read outside newspapers will still have reached you through the agency of a typewriter or something even more primitive, like a human hand holding a pen.

U

Unique

This word is already used colloquially to mean something like 'unusual', and many are the denunciations that its appearance with qualifiers (*rather unique, very unique*) has excited. This misuse is so notorious among the almost-literate that, like the split infinitive, anything reminiscent of it is best avoided. The phrase, or a phrase like, *rather unique*, meaning something of the order of 'unique in some ways though perhaps not in others', seems to me defensible in usage and semantics, but I would not advise anybody to use it who fancies a quiet life. It would be no less risky to mention those long-dead pedants who once campaigned against *almost invariably* on similar grounds.

Unities

A good deal was heard of these when I was a lad, nothing much now except retrospectively, historically. The unity of time was preserved if the entire action of a play (fable, story, novel) occupied no more than twenty-four hours, that of place if changes of scene were small and unobtrusive, that of action if everything introduced bore on the main action. Only the third has scope as well as substance, and the example of *Hamlet* suggests its inadequacy. Nevertheless any thorough critique of that play would have to take large account of its neglect of the unity of action, though probably not under that name.

University

What constitutes a university, and how that might differ from what constitutes a polytechnic or other establishment for vocational training, it is not my present business to expound. Nevertheless it cannot be said too often that education is one thing and instruction, however worthy, necessary and incidentally or momentarily educative, another.

Up to a point, Lord Copper

I wonder how many users of this expression could say where it comes from. Not a majority, to judge by the number of people who seem to think it registers tepid agreement, as the first four words by themselves would, with Lord Copper being named as part of some exotic ritual, perhaps propitiatory in derivation. I have said 'Up to a point' in conversation before now and set a dunce or two mechanically intoning 'Lord Copper' as if to complete a mantra. I was reminded of the lady who, having once heard somebody say 'Surprise, surprise' but not noticed the sarcastic intention, said brightly, 'Oh, what a lovely surprise, surprise' on being offered a chocolate.

In fact 'Up to a point, Lord Copper' was said by an underling to the great newspaper proprietor in order to register the strongest disagreement thought to be safe. See *Scoop*, by Evelyn Waugh. Outside its context the phrase may be misleading and should be dropped.

V

Viable

This word was once applied only to foetuses and meant 'capable of being brought to (full) term', and when metaphorically used should still observe the connection. In fact *viable* should be dropped altogether, not for any elaborate semantic reason but simply because it has taken the fancy of every trendy little twit on the look-out for a posh word for *feasible, practicable*.

Virile

This is a few years ago now, but I cannot resist dropping a reminder that, attacked by collective illiteracy more severely than usual, journalists forgot that the word descended not very far from the Latin *vir*, man (as opposed to a woman) and meant by rights 'having masculine vigour or strength', not just 'vigorous, full of beans', and so it was not all right to say, among other things, that an old lady was still virile at the age of ninety-three. So far, so entirely predictable, but nobody could have guessed Fowler's comment that in this case the reporter had probably associated *virility* 'with *viridus* green, not *vir* man, and was thinking of a green old age'. End of note.

Visitor's London

This usage, which could be called a false possessive, is an import from the USA, along with *England's London*. The latter takes care of those who, hearing perhaps of Buckingham Palace in London, need to be told that neither London, Ontario nor London, Ohio is meant, though *London, England* used to do that job efficiently enough without a vexatious apostrophe.

England's London may be considered a solecism or a misnomer, but *England's Helicon* is neither. This is the title of a book published in 1600, an anthology containing poems by Sidney, Spenser, Drayton and others. The original Helicon was a Greek mountain sacred to the Muses, who had a temple there. The phrase *England's Helicon* is thus not semantically on all fours with *England's London*. The one says something like 'if there were a Mt Helicon in England, its native Muses would surely smile on the contents of this volume,' whereas the other, like California's Death Valley, Pisa's Leaning Tower and the rest, does not even make a claim to ownership but just says limply that such-and-such a thing is to be found in such-and-such a place.

For all that, expressions like *Pepys's London* are defensible. They do not claim any kind of proprietorship but are obvious shorthand for *London as so-and-so knew it*. But if an adjective exists it should be used in such contexts, *Victorian* not *Victoria's London*.

Watershed

Here I think is a lonely instance of a vulgarisation being turned back on itself. Once, a watershed was a line of separation between waters flowing to different rivers or basins or seas; the second element, *scheide*, of the German word from which *watershed* is taken is indeed cognate with the English verb *shed* and means 'boundary'. Next, *watershed* was popularised and misapplied to mean a catchment area ('the school became a watershed for all children born in this part of South London'). Finally, the word reverted to its old hydrographical sense. Or did so in effect; more accurately, perhaps, the popularisation faded away and the true technical meaning carried on as before.

Weave

The *weave* in the fabric sense and the *weave* in the moving (to and fro) sense are different words, each with its separate line of descent from an earlier stage of the language. So anyone who says anything like 'The car *wove* its way through the lines of traffic' is guilty of a solecism. The preterite of *weave*-moving is *weaved*.

Welsh rarebit

The *rarebit* part of this expression is not genuine. The *Welsh* part is, or more nearly is, recalling as it does a now-forgotten era when the Welsh people were supposed to have a passion for cheese. I have no way of knowing how truly this reflects Welsh dietetic habits in, let us say, the seventeenth century, but it seems plausible that an indigent pastoral people would have snapped up all the eatables they could find, very much including cheese, which lends itself to being turned into a hot dish for the family with the aid of a dab of butter and a little ale and pepper and salt.

Clearly, the English called the result a Welsh rabbit partly in jest, partly as a sneer – more jest than sneer, probably, since over the years the English have always been much more friendly to the Welsh than to the Scots or Irish. To call a lump of toasted cheese a rabbit shows the same bantering spirit as, more recently, a mishit at cricket got dubbed a Chinese cut, less commonly a Czechoslovakian one.

The phrase *Welsh rabbit* dates from the earlier eighteenth century. *Welsh rarebit* is much later, and no evidence exists of the independent use of *rarebit* to mean delicacy or anything else. The *COD* gives it as the result of popular etymology. With all respect, I think the *COD* is wrong here. I think that *rarebit* is more likely to be a juvenile form of political correctness, in that it anticipates and forestalls objection by the Welsh, none of whom is known to have bothered to complain, to something just conceivably derogatory to them like *Welsh rabbit*. But I have no strong or even very definite feelings on the point.

I had to laugh, though, when I once picked up the menu at a posh restaurant, the sort of menu where they print the name of the chap whose recipe they say they use, and saw among the afters 'Welsh Rabbit Llewelyn Rhys'. In my experience Welshmen rarely miss jokes wherever they may be aimed.

What x is (all) about

It seems important not to spend a moment more than strictly necessary in denouncing this fearful gobbet of trend. Anybody who speaks or writes to the effect that anything is what anything, anything at all from aardvarks to zymotics, is *about*, especially *all about*, deserves exclusion from the ways and habitations of mankind forthwith and without possibility of remission in the foreseeable future.

Whizz

English spelling is littered with intrusive letters that may have been pronounced at some earlier stage but are not, or not everywhere, these days. Thus initial K in words like *knight* and *knee* was probably still sounded by some speakers in some areas in the eighteenth century; initial P in words like *psychology* and perhaps *pterodactyl* is supposed to have lasted well into the twentieth, although I myself, born in 1922, never heard it. Nowadays initial P in such words is sounded no more, with the annoying result among others that *psychosis*, gross mental derangement, sounds just the same as *sycosis*, a form of shaving-rash. Others have gone too at less measurable times, like the H in *ghastly* and *ghost*, which was actually sneaked in by early printers and never pronounced. The case for its retention in writing, however, has become a definite part of the whole case against spelling reform.

One letter formerly sounded everywhere is the H in imitatives like *whizz* and *whack*, relative-interrogatives like *which* and *what*, and plenty of other words like *wheat* and *whet.* In all cases the H-sound precedes the W-sound and ancestral forms show the H coming first too in written records. (Indeed to pronounce such an H immediately *after* a W is not very practicable for normal English-speakers, however straightforward it may be for some others.) That particular H is still naturally sounded in parts of Scotland, Ireland and America, at any rate among older speakers. Irish English especially, perhaps like the Irish language, was always heavily aspirated, and in the supposed rustic or below-stairs variant *phwat* for *what* we can hear an attempt to indicate such an initial cluster of sounds. The Scottish consonant *ch*, as in *loch*, might have come closer, but that would have entailed explanation and some real interest on the reader's part.

The most important word in the foregoing paragraph is 'naturally', and in this matter as in others naturalness, lack of self-consciousness, must set such speakers at a priceless advantage over those who speak as they think they should. No affectation is easier to detect than a phoney HW beginning to *wh-* words, with its taint of such cobwebbed nooks as elocution classes. Let us hope that we shall soon hear no more of this artificiality. I only hope I am wrong when I uneasily sense its impending revival among self-admiring broadcasters.

Whom

It has become safe to say that, except in funeral addresses and the like, or as a joke, *whom* is no longer heard from speakers of English. The word is found in formal prose, sometimes when *who* is required, as in *Unfortunately I had not then heard whom he was.* On other occasions *who* is found in prose formal enough to make some readers feel that *whom*, if perhaps not positively required, would be preferable as more respectful, as in *I was then presented to His Royal High-*

ness, who I felt was known to me already from our previous meeting.

Here no rule of thumb is possible for the writer, but it may be helpful to keep on the look-out for *whom* territory and at other times try to forget the word altogether.

Whose

The theoretical lexicon of the English language contains no relative pronoun of the inanimate in a genitive sense. In other and perhaps less forbidding words, you can talk about 'the lady, *whose* figure was ample and genuine', but not, theoretically, 'the lady's figure, *whose* amplitude and genuineness were equally obvious'; you have to say something like 'the lady's figure, the amplitude and genuineness *of which* were equally obvious'.

It is now over sixty years since Fowler was denouncing this 'rule' as about as helpful as the one that forbade putting a preposition at the end of a sentence. He produced a real example with no fewer than twelve words in the *which* clause before the reader got to *which* itself. But now, sixty years later as I say, writers are still refusing to allow *which* its full natural freedom and still insisting on writing about 'the dictionary, the peerless scholarship and consequent utter reliability in trying circumstances of which have assisted our task' and refusing to write about 'the dictionary, whose peerless scholarship and consequent utter reliability in trying circumstances have assisted our task'. Nobody who has ever had to string half a dozen sentences together will think that the licence to write the second kind of sentence instead of the first is not worth bothering about.

-wise

There are a few words with *-wise* incorporated in them so firmly that the fusion has become an established word, such as *likewise, otherwise, clockwise, anticlockwise*, perhaps *crabwise*. Elsewhere, for instance in *moneywise* ('the project is sound moneywise') or in *clubwise*, say ('the soldier used his rifle clubwise'), a kind of promiscuity seems about to rage. General ridicule or weariness may quell it; nothing else seems likely to.

Womanese

It has long been noticed, by members of both sexes in their different ways, that men and women speak discrete languages, or more precisely they speak closely related variants of a single language. Each variant is well enough understood across the sexual divide, but attempts to treat the two as one are as unproductive as any other chimera about the essential sameness of men and women. The word *reasonable*, to take a familiar case, changes meaning with the sex of its user. So a wife might say of her husband that it was not reasonable of him to expect her to be reasonable on some stated occasion and be understood, not as one making a mildly cynical, moderately impartial, worldly-wise remark on a difference between the two sexes, but as putting forward a serious, valid complaint about typical male insensitivity – putting it to another female, naturally.

No doubt I have already come too far to be safe. I had better take refuge behind the rock-hard factual observation that, unlike most men, women are always getting set phrases wrong. This propensity of theirs was noted at least as far back as the works of Somerset Maugham (1874–1965), if not much further in the character of Mrs Malaprop in Sheridan's *The Rivals* of 1775, whose nice derangement of epitaphs may have struck many auditors as not close enough for discomfort but never, surely, as being put into the mouth or a character of the wrong sex. It is worth noting not only as required but also as accurate that Mrs Malaprop's mistakes are nearly enough on target to be, like so many of this type, inners rather than outers or hopeless misses. You can always guess at once what she nearly said.

My ignorance of foreign languages is far too deep for me even to conjecture what female behaviour there might be. The novels and stories of Peter DeVries, however, from *Tunnel of Love* (1954) onwards, make it clear that such divergences or variations (or whatever one is to call them) of self-expression thrive in the land of the free. There and only there, possibly, could a wife have said to a husband in reference to some third party, 'No, you're wrong, he's not a profound character, at least only on the surface. Deep down he's shallow.' This is perhaps not exactly a malapropism but that it is a specimen of womanese will be doubted by no normal male who has talked to a normal female for more than five minutes. Such a one will, if he is any good, have seen that examples of womanese and of how men respond to them capture a pair of truths about the sexes in a way that no discourse in run-of-the-mill English could.

So to our own time and place. I fill out this pioneering study by reproducing a string of such cases as listed in a novel of 1995. Note the wide range of styles ventured into. All phrases quoted are warranted truthful instances of womanese, presented flat. *Vicious snowball. Quicksand wit. Up gum street. Beyond contempt. On its death legs. Hubbub of activity. When it came down to the crunch. Greaseboat. He lost his top* and *she blew her rag.* And *I was talking aloud* – once, just once, but once.

It is not extraordinary that the extraterrestrial origin of women was a recurrent theme of science fiction, though I have never seen their imperfect grasp of their native language put forward as one more piece of evidence.

Wrath, wroth

These words for (righteous) anger and (righteously) angry are now too archaic for use in serious conversation: 'poet., rhet. or joc.' says *COD* against *wrath*. Even so, the noun appears in solemn places like newspaper headlines, this very day in the front-page banner of a popular daily to describe the Tory backbench response to some of the Chancellor's budget proposals. The biblical and other associations of *wrath* make it suitable for a more serious and more disinterested emotion than that denoted by *anger* on its own.

Pronounce *wrath* to rhyme with *moth*, and *wroth*, now surely an obsolete word, to rhyme with *both*. Avoid them equally in whatever you may say or write yourself.

Writing: repetitions

Philip Larkin once said he admired Hemingway for his work-habits more than any other writer. 'You know how when you start in the morning it's like getting blood out of a stone to begin with, with lots of time spent just staring at the blank paper and going out for a pee and thank God when the phone rings, and then you gradually speed up so that after an hour or more the stuff's coming quite easily, well of course I don't mean *easily*, just a bit faster – you get that, don't you? I think probably most writers do. Well, our Ernie's no exception there, only when he gets to the point where he starts speeding up, he stops writing.'

'For the day?'

'He sometimes goes back before the first evening drink like some people and starts again.'

'I don't see much to admire in any of that. He's cutting out the only time he might actually enjoy writing if he's ever going to.'

'That's what's admirable. Any fool can wallow in what he does without really trying.'

It used to be fashionable to say of things like Hemingway's alleged work-habits that there was something 'very English' about going on as if only what you rather disliked doing had a chance of producing anything remotely worthwhile. But it is no secret that Hemingway was not merely American but one of a characteristically self-conscious kind, about as un-English as he could get without ceasing to speak and write in that language. One wonders if there may not be something about that language that tends to enforce Protestantism, even Puritanism, on the user. But again, it was the English (and Protestant) Larkin who said or wrote, as a memento to all literary persons, 'No one will enjoy reading what you have not enjoyed writing.' After all, it could only have been a Frenchman or Irishman who held the view that to write in the expectation of being enjoyed denoted a certain simplicity of mind.

When I look back over my own first drafts, something I very rarely do except while constructing a fair copy, I notice several passages that seem to have originated in that early, costive period of a day's stint. They are distinguishable by the toilsome conscientiousness with which typing errors are corrected, unnecessary words x-ed out, repetitions avoided. Paragraphs first-drafted later in the day let such blemishes stand as their perpetrator confidently entrusts their rectification to some time in the future. Nearer the start, writers are nervous, feeling their way, killing time by performing necessary but postponable tasks, doing the mechanised equivalent of circling with their elbows before actually putting pen to paper. This sort of explanation for slow beginnings appeals to me quite as much as any literary-doctrinal farrago.

Both ways of looking at matutinal awkwardness, however, agree that unintentional repetition is the most pernicious of errors. There could be no clearer sign of a writer

who is incompetent, lazy, hurried, preoccupied, demoralised. Two of the finest poems in our language are almost
ruined right at the start, where their early drafts presumably
began. Goldsmith's *Deserted Village* notoriously kicks off
with an irremediable and destructive piece of self-repetition
that hardly needs emphasising italica:

> *Ill* fares the land, to hastening *ills* a prey,
> Where wealth accumulates, and men decay . . .

Did Johnson, who according to Boswell wrote the last four
lines of the poem, never mention its disastrous opening?
All the reader can do now is hold his nose and hurry on to
less noisome pastures, as must the reader of Blake's 'London',
which opens with the stanza:

> I wander through each chartered street
> Near where the chartered Thames does flow,
> And *mark* in every face I meet
> *Marks* of weakness, *marks* of woe.

Here the repetition of 'chartered', whatever it means exactly,
like the repetition of 'every' in the next stanza, is unmistakably purposeful or advertent, that of 'mark(s)' unmistakably
negligent and inadvertent. Both poets were too eager to get
on with the poem concerned or the next one to reread their
first drafts to any purpose, though with Blake at least one
cannot be sure that some pissy notion of spontaneity may have
stood in the way of unarguably necessary correction. But then
if those who think like Hemingway, who incidentally often
repeated words on purpose, sense a possibly fruitful difference
between what their nine and eleven o'clock selves produce,
perhaps they are right. I find it most unlikely.

Before sitting down to this entry I half-intended it to
be an introduction of some sort to an illustrated account,
not of how to write well, but of what non-grammatical

faults to look out for. I would show a passage of fiction full of assonances, excessive alliteration, etc., and point these out. No great thought was required to convince me that here was a region in which a feigned example hath not anything like as much force to teach as a true example. A useful true example would take some finding and be impossibly long and diffuse even if found; a feigned example could never seem natural and so could not be useful. Nevertheless the point is too important to be brushed aside with a mention and an apology. A detailed generalisation will have to do instead.

The fundamental generalisation is clearly that an inadvertent repetition, or anything that could reasonably be mistaken for one, is bad. I have counted six kinds of harmful repetition.

1. Rhyme. As in You have to pay on the appointed day. 'Rich rhyme' is just as bad, as in It must be conceded that we have succeeded.
2. Likeness of vowel sounds falling short of actual rhyme, as in The bill must be paid on the appointed day.
3. Excessive alliteration, as in Public pressure compels private persons to pay as promptly as postal collections permit. Three words running with the same initial letter or sound is probably the limit in ordinary prose. Read out what you have first-drafted and see.
4. Persistent verse-like rhythms, as in Many letters posted in the middle of the day never reach their destination till a day or two has passed. Victorian writers, especially Dickens, were liable to write blank verse (printed as prose) in passages of strong emotion.
5. Too many words of the same form, as those that end in -ing, -y (not least -ly) and -tion. Prose that appears at first sight to be just boring often harbours too many of these. I try as a rough rule not to use any of them more than once or twice in a sentence.

6. Same word reappearing. Particularly easy to fall into when the word in question is common in more than one meaning, as *look*, *like*, etc. Very common words, as *any*, *after*, etc., can probably be repeated.

Like other kinds of fault, this one is more readily detected by reading a passage aloud, but whatever faculty it may be that helps the writer not to repeat words and sounds is not evenly distributed. Philip Larkin was helped by a fastidious temperament and ferocious conscientiousness, and was able to boast, justifiably I think, that the only words in *Jill* to be repeated were of the status of *and* or *the*. For all that, he perpetrated an ungainly repetition many years later, near the end of one of his best and most finely crafted poems, 'Going, Going':

> Most things are never meant,
> This won't be, most likely . . .

I refrained from telling him that Tennyson would never have let that through.

Another writer who evidently had a faultless ear was Chesterton. Even in his journalism, often written against time, he never inadvertently repeats a sound. Or if he does, I may well have missed it. My own non-repetitive gifts are all of the will, and the will fluctuates. Quite likely I have perpetrated the ineptitude in this very article, but to be rebuked for such inconsistency cuts no ice with me. I chime in with the warrant officer's plea, 'Don't do as I do, do as I say.'

Y

Ye olde

Grammarians will tell you that the letter at the front of *ye olde* is not a Y but a representation of an obsolete letter, an *edh* or *eth*, that looked a bit like a Y. The *edh* or *eth* sounded like a *th* and the whole phrase should be pronounced indistinguishably from *the old*. This is the sort of thing that gets grammarians a bad name. It may not be the funniest jest in the world, but a lot of people have at least used and understood expressions like *ye olde lettering*, meaning perhaps Gothic type or script. Here *ye olde* must be pronounced *yee oldie* if the meaning, along with a possible gleam of humour, is not to be lost. Similarly, when claiming the authorship of Shakespeare's plays Marlowe must say, 'Teehee It was me all yee [not *the*] time.'

Yoo and oo

This is a question of pure pronunciation and therefore boring or beside the point to a minority of readers, not in my estimate a large minority. Grown men will come to blows no less readily over the correct pronunciation of *heinous*, for example, than about who really won the last war.

I had better say immediately that no one is, perhaps no one could be, totally consistent about how he or she pronounces the first syllable of *beautiful*, *suitable*, *dewdrop*, *bluebottle*, *glue-pot*, *fluted* and other such words, and just as immediately that I am an elderly Londoner of lower-middle-class origin.

Now in many phonetic situations the speaker has a choice between a *yoo* sound and a plain *oo* sound. Which choice that speaker makes depends on several things, including place of origin, age and social class. The reaction of hearers is similarly influenced, with some such overall result as the following:

To say *yoo* where others would say plain *oo* may strike some hearers as prissy, old-fashioned and over-educated. Thus my sons, born in the 1940s, ridicule me for saying *syootable* and *syoo* for *suitable* and *sue*; they would use the plain *oo*. Similarly, it sounds old-fashioned and provincial to me when I hear a speaker in Wales talk about a *flyoot* (flute) or a *scryoo* (screw) or the colour *blyoo*. And if I were to come across an upper-class speaker who said *flyoot* and *lyoot* (lute) and *glyoo* (glue) I should conclude among other things that he was very old indeed, or at least old-fashioned.

Those who say *bootiful* and *foo* (few), if any still do outside Norfolk turkey commercials, also seem to me old-fashioned and provincial. No doubt people like my sons would respond similarly, though perhaps more incredulously. I myself regard those who would say *tootor* (tutor) or *toon* as hopelessly down-market.

A rough consensus seems to emerge whereby pronunciations with *yoo* strike some hearers as affected, while pronunciations with *oo* strike some others as bucolic or vulgar. Such displays of mild but inflammable prejudice strike me as peculiarly English.

Glossary

In compiling this book I have constantly had forced on me afresh the extent to which the subject of English grammar has in this country been founded on the subject of Latin. The two languages are actually not very similar, and Latin is now rarely taught anywhere, yet it has left strong traces in our grammatical vocabulary and modes of thought. This has brought me here a dilemma between being too Latinate and not Latinate enough, between saying too much to maintain a sense of direction and saying too little to be clear. I have tried to compromise, but my readers are bound to feel a loss of certainty here and there, especially in this Glossary. I can only ask their indulgence.

allegory. An account of one thing in the guise of another. Example: *Pilgrim's Progress* is an *allegory* of human life. *The Faerie Queen* is a series of *allegories*. Kafka's stories are largely *allegorical*.

aorist. Pronounced (when I last used to word) AIRist. The name of a generic past tense in classical Greek, from a word meaning 'indefinite'; not a perfect, not an imperfect, not a pluperfect, just past. Normally used as a classy synonym for preterite or past historic, but nicely applied to an American idiom whereby people say, 'The upstate train just came in,' meaning it came in a few seconds or a couple of minutes ago and is quite likely still in. A British speaker would have had to use the perfect and say, 'The train's just come in.'

assimilation. Making one sound more like another, usually the one that follows. For instance, the word *impossible* started life as a combination of two words of which the first was *in* meaning *not*, but the *n* became *m* by assimilation.

Uneducated speech in London and elsewhere is full of assimilations, and this tendency is probably on the increase. I cannot clearly remember hearing somebody talk about *a dime breed* (meaning 'a dying breed') more than ten or twenty years ago. We also reportedly have the proper names *Samamfa* (Samantha) and *Scumforpe* (Scunthorpe).

Cases. See also article on CASE, where it is suggested among other things that some English words in a sentence have cases even though these are not detectable as inflections.

The traditional six cases affecting nouns, pronouns and adjectives are as follows:

nominative, the naming case. A noun forming the subject of a sentence or, if an adjective, part of that subject. Example in English: The *cat* sat on the mat. Also: The *black* cat is mine.

vocative, the calling case. In all English and nearly all Latin nouns the same in appearance as the nominative. Used when addressing or invoking some person or abstraction. Examples: Call me tomorrow, *Percy*. O *Liberty*, what crimes are committed in thy name!

accusative, the picking-out case. A noun etc. forming the object of a sentence or something aimed at. Examples: Caesar will attack *Rome*. Percy will perhaps go to *Wigan* for the weekend.

genitive, the ownership or source case, corresponding to *of* or *from*. Can be distinguished by *'s* if the owner or source is a person. Examples: *Bill's* nose. The adverse vote was *Bill's*.

dative, the giving case, corresponding to *to* or *for* and expressing indirect or recipient. Examples: Give *me* your hand. I showed *Jenkins* who was master.

ablative, sometimes called instrumental, the taking-away or

254

what-did-it case, corresponding to source or cause. Examples: The chutney came *from India*. He was killed *by criminals*.

caesura. Sizz-YOO-ruh. A cut or cutting. A technical term in Greek or Latin versification, now usually meaning a heavy break in a line of English verse. Example, from a sonnet to Shakespeare: *Others abide our question. Thou art free.* Caesura at full stop after *question.*

chiasmus. Kigh-AZZmus. Two phrases going together of which the second inverts the order of the first. Example: *I cannot dig; to beg I am ashamed.* Named after the Greek letter *khi* or *chi*, which is shaped like a (St Andrew's) cross.

clause. A sentence, or in phrases like *relative clause, subordinate clause*, a distinct part of one.

cognate. A word descended from an ancestor it shares with another in a different language is said to be *cognate* with it, or *a cognate* of it. Example: *The word father in English and the word vater in German are cognate(s)*. Neither is directly descended from the other, a provision that rules out, say, *arid* as cognate with Latin *aridus*, its direct ancestor.

concessive clause. One introduced by *although* or equivalent.

consecutive clause. One introduced by *with the consequence that* or equivalent.

dissimilation. Making one sound less like another; cf. *assimilation*. The *COD* example is *cinnamon*, at an earlier stage *cinnamom*. Repeated consonants, especially perhaps labials, can be difficult to say. I remember a neighbour who could never get her tongue round the second half of *chrysanthemum*.

English, Old, Middle and Modern English. In the popular mind, or that of most well-wishers of respectful dealings with our language, Old English, often styled old English, runs from the beginning to when people began to spell properly (apart from a few olde-isms like *smoaking* and *musick*), and modern English describes the rest, perhaps with the exception of Middle English which is to do with Chaucer. The reality is more definite without being quite satisfactorily defined.

Old English was the language of England that ran from the beginnings to about AD 1150. Its general resemblance to present-day English is small, in fact if speakers of it could be reconstituted we should not be able to understand their speech, nor they ours, though a written transcript might give us some inkling. Some little Old English survives in manuscript. It seems to me too scanty and remote for any artistic merit to have survived in it, but it is of linguistic interest, naturally.

Middle English runs from about 1150 to about 1500. It contains many words that, often with differences in spelling and pronunciation, survive in the present-day language, many others too that have changed their meaning or altogether gone out of use. There are very large remains of Middle English literature and other writing and its greatest exponent was undoubtedly Geoffrey Chaucer (*c.* 1340–1400), though others are important.

Modern English is taken to have begun about AD 1500. Thus Shakespeare wrote entirely in it, which does not mean that what he and his contemporaries wrote is always readily intelligible to us or to our contemporaries. For one thing, the language has gone on changing since then.

By the way, only a barbarian talks of old English when Elizabethan or Jacobean or other 'old-fashioned English' is meant.

figures of speech. These were once all the rage, and I can remember learning the difference between *hypallage* and *synecdoche*, and much good it did me. The two best known in English today are *simile* and *metaphor*. A simile is a comparison openly expressed as such. Example: *The ship goes through the sea (in the same way) as a plough goes through the soil.* A metaphor is a concentrated comparison that avoids *like* or *as*. Example: *The ship ploughs (through) the sea.* *Metaphor* is also used less closely to mean a fanciful but on consideration apt comparison, as in *This suggestion gave him food for thought.*

Other figures of speech include *hyperbole*, exaggeration for emphasis, sometimes flowery, as in *A thousand thanks!*, often colloquial and thoughtless, as in *I'm dying for a smoke*; *litotes* or *meiosis*, rhetorical understatement, as in *He was not sorry to rest a while*; *personification*, which needs no explaining: *rhetorical question*, one to which the answer is self-evident, as in *Who's like us?*: *zeugma*, the yoking-together of two nouns or noun phrases by a single verb, etc., as in *She left in high dudgeon and a minicab.* The last is an example of what Fowler would have called a battered ornament and was never very funny.

gerund. This is a verbal noun. Example: the art of *loving.*

gerundive. This is a verbal adjective. Example: my *loving* wife.
Fowler says there is no gerundive in English, only a participle. He writes 2000 words on the gerund alone. In my experience you will not get very far with gerund/gerundive unless you know Latin, nor a great deal further if you do.

heroic. Heroic poetry is epic; *heroic verse* is strictly Greek or Latin hexameters or English blank verse; the *heroic couplet* is two rhyming lines, each of five iambic feet (see below); *heroic virtues*, or heroic virtues, are fortitude and loyalty and whatever else you please.

hexameter. A six-measure line of Greek or Latin verse. The hexameter has been tried in English but never successfully.

ictus. Metrical *ictus* is the regular beat of the verse, falling in the normal English iambic line on the even-numbered syllables.

loan word. The English word *chauffeur* is spoken of as a *loan word* from the French, an unsatisfactory term because real loans have to be paid back. But the usage is well entrenched and the only other that comes to mind, whereby *chauffeur* is spoken of as a *borrowing* from the French, offers the same defective image. Never mind.

locative. The locative case of a noun (if one exists) indicates the place *where* something-or-other. It is an extra to the familiar six cases. Although there are vestiges of it in Latin, the locative had no forms of its own and altogether is something to have heard of rather than taken account of.

metre and rhythm. Metre is regular and regularly recurring, as in *iambic metre* where the metric stress alternates uniformly all through; *rhythm* varies from line to line with the run of the words and depends on their meaning. So the *metre* of *Bare ruined choirs, where late the sweet birds sang* would go ti-tum-ti-tum-ti-tum-ti-tum-ti-tum; the *rhythm* would go tum-tum-ti-tum (pause) tum-tum-ti-tum-tum-tum; if I had you here I could demonstrate in five seconds. Playing off the two kinds of stress against each other gives English poetry its characteristic effect.

metrical feet. The names of these in English are based on the usage in Latin. The commonest of these is the *iambus*, a light stress followed by a heavy one, example *return*. Others include the *trochee*, heavy followed by light, as *brother*; the *dactyl*, heavy followed by two light, as *auditor*; the *anapaest*, two light followed by one heavy, as *cigarette*.

object, direct and *indirect.* That which is directly, or indirectly, affected by the verb in a sentence. In *Lend me your ears*, for instance, *your ears* (thing lent) is the direct object and *me* (person lent to) the indirect object.

pathetic fallacy. Anybody who happens not to know this phrase already, as it were, is ludicrously distant from being able to work out what it means, and the thing itself has now been all but silenced by ridicule; nevertheless duty still calls. Ruskin originally coined the phrase. In Fowler's words the so-called fallacy means 'the tendency to credit nature with human emotions', and 'the wind gave a howl of disappointed fury at its victim's escape' is often given as an example. Adjectives applied to the sea are especially fraught with this danger, or said to be.

penultimate. Means 'last but one', not, as increasingly in USA, 'the *really* last, last in a big way'.

prosody. The rules of verse composition, chiefly involving a list of metres and how to use them, derived from study of existing practice.

saga. Technically, a medieval Scandinavian prose narrative, involving historical facts. More recently a long historical narrative in fictional form ('The Forsyte Saga') or a sequence of real-life events (the Nixon saga).

subjunctive. Known in full as the subjunctive mood. The last word is not good here, not illuminating. *Mode*, not originally connected with it, is better. The reference is to the form or forms of verb showing how it is to be taken, as an expression of fact, command, wish, etc.

The further one ventures into this subject without benefit of Latin, the more likely one is to get bogged down. It is more practical to avoid any involvement. This is possible if two simple rules are observed, as follows:

1. Avoid an *if*-clause or a virtual *if*-clause when using any part

of the verb *to be* in any capacity, however apparently trivial.
2. Be careful with any American writings, which often indulge in subjunctive forms, especially if the context seems precise or public in any way. Do not imitate them. If necessary, mentally translate them into familiar indicative English.

Any sentence with a subjunctive form in it (e.g. 'it was decided that we adjourn' rather than 'that we *should* adjourn') is suspect. N.B.: The above rules are not flippant or satirical.

tense. The *tense* of a verb marks the time its action takes place, and the word ultimately descends from Latin *tempus*, 'time', so present, future, past. This simple scheme would give every verb a maximum of three tenses. Unfortunately a verbal form can also indicate whether the action is complete or not and other subtleties. Thus a Latin verb usually has a present sense, *I go*; a simple future, *I shall go*; an imperfect (incomplete past), *I was going*; a perfect, past action completed, *I have gone* or *I went*; a future perfect, *I shall have gone*; and a pluperfect, i.e. more than perfect, *I had gone*. It would make good sense to forget the whole of the last sentence instantly, were it not that some writers give versions of the names of Latin tenses when referring to the very different modes used in English to denote the time or completeness etc. of an action, the two being quite disparate languages except in some points of vocabulary. This abbreviated sketch of the matter is intended to help you find your way from one language to another when Latin expressions describe English usages.

Note that the *preterite*, a term not used with Latin verbs, is the historic past tense, like Latin perfect in the second aspect described above, *I went*.

voice. This sounds formidable, according to the *COD* the 'set of forms of a verb showing relation of the subject to the action (ACTIVE, PASSIVE, MIDDLE, *voice*); verb in this form.' Pfui! Except for its occurrence in Ancient Greek, there is no middle voice worth bothering about, and an example of a verb-form in the active, 'doing', voice is *I love*, and an example of a verb-form in the passive, 'acted upon', voice is *I am loved*, and that is that.

Index

Index